American Decline

The Moral and Political Unravelling of a Nation

Innocent A. Emechete

Table of Contents

Copyright

DEDICATION

I wish to dedicate this book to all the innocent children killed through abortion and all the unsuspecting innocent children lured into alternative lifestyles as well as those who committed suicide when they realized they have been deceived by adults who were supposed to protect them.

INTRODUCTION

The United States of America has a long and interesting history. She has a vast expanse of land stretching from the Pacific Ocean in the West to the Atlantic Ocean in the East, Canada in the north and Mexico in the south. Before the first immigrants arrived in the area under discussion, the different tribes of Indians, generally called Native Americans, were there, probably more than 20,000 years before. According to Wikipedia, there were about five hundred and seventy-four (574) nations or tribes or native American tribes before the Europeans came into the territory we now call north and south America or the Americas. The native Americans can be divided into four major groups:

1. The American Indian;

2. The Alaskan Native;

3. The Canadian Indian and

4. The Latin American Indian.

They have their unique cultures, traditions and languages. The ten major tribes are

1. the Cherokee;

2. the Navajo;

3. the Choctaw;

4. the Chippewa;

5. the Sioux;

6. the Apache;

7. the Blackfeet;

8. the Creek;

9. the Iroquois and

10. the Lumbee tribes.

Apart from the Native Americans, the United States of America is a collection of many peoples and languages. The migration into the United States of America started from Europe in the 16th century. They came from Great Britain, Portugal, Spain, Netherlands and France. Later more immigrants came from Sweden, Finland, Estonia, Norway, Russia, Poland to mention just a few. Between 1492 and 1640 there were about 446,000 European immigrants in the United States of America. There were many different native American cultures and languages before another swarm of immigrants from Europe came with multiples of cultures and languages. The immigrants were scattered all over the territory in clusters known as colonies then. At first people of the same culture and language stayed together. For a while different groups clustered in different geographical areas according to their cultures and languages. Some of the explorers came just to trade with the Natives for profit while some came to colonize and stay. Some came because of religious persecution or oppression from their home governments while others came as laborers to make money in the plantations in America. Some inhabitants of the new land also were forced to come as slaves from Africa while others came as convicts from European prisons to work in the plantations. It is estimated that between the late 1610s and the industrial revolution, from fifty thousand (50,000) to one hundred and twenty thousand (120,000) British convicts were shipped to their colonies in America. Apart from these convicts, there were yet another group, indentured servants from Great Britain to the colonies for work in the plantations for money. At the time when life in the British colonies was getting better than life in Great Britain itself, a number of young British people had a strong desire to go to the colonies in America to work. But a lot of them could not afford the fare to migrate to America. The cotton and tobacco plantation owners, who needed them, had to enter into an agreement with them to pay their fare in exchange for between four (4) to seven (7) years of service on the plantations at the end of which the plantation owner would give them a piece of land to own and cultivate. That was a good deal for both sides. About 50 per cent of British immigrants came under this arrangement.

The British Colonizers were willing to stay under the British Crown and the British Government was happy to provide them British military protection from the French and Spanish powers. Even when that threat was no longer there, the British Government still wanted the colonies to exist for the British Crown for obvious reasons. As British subjects in America, the British Crown was getting a lot of advantages from the farm owners through taxation. While the British Government was getting revenue from America, the British people in America had no representation in the Parliament. This lack of participation in the British Parliament would eventually cause friction between them and finally become the reason for the colonies' quest for autonomy. That request for autonomy would result in a war of independence from the British government. After that war of Independence, the United States of America finally became an independent nation from the British Crown and became a Sovereign Nation in 1776.

As the immigrants came, they established their religion in their colonies. There were the Dutch Calvinists, the British Puritans, the Dutch Quakers/Amsterdam Quakers/Dutch Mennonite/Amish, the Methodists, the French Huguenots, the British/Dutch Baptists and later the Irish Catholics. In areas where different colonies lived together for some business ventures or trade cooperation and relationships, their different religions coexisted because religion was also important to each group. America became the hot spot of people from all over the world with different languages, cultures and religions living together apparently peacefully. That variety became the greatest asset of the United States. Variety brought innovation and collaboration that made America great and unique. Immigration of people from all over the world to America assembled the best and the worst in one place and made the United States the unique country that it became. That was then.

That which made America great also contributed to some of its handicaps today. The makeup of the United States of America provided a constant polarity in the structural, daring attitudes, political and religious aspects of the nation. In the formulation of her Constitution, certain freedoms were enshrined. These freedoms which came from a common experience of the immigrants from Europe were rational and practical for peaceful coexistence of the different peoples and languages and faiths.

These same good principles and guidance that made America great later became potential problems for the United States.

After the war for independence, there was a civil war between the Union Army (North) and the Confederate Army (South) over the abolition of slave trade. The South depended heavily on slave labor for the farms and was ready to go to war to maintain slavery. But President Lincoln's Emancipation Proclamation freed more than 3 million enslaved blacks in the Confederate states on January 1, 1863. That caused the enlistment into the Union Army of about 180,000 blacks by the end of the civil war. Further President Lincoln proposed that blacks deserved the right to vote as well, and he was assassinated three days later.

The issues of the North and the South, black and white, free and slave, republican and democrat, have become issues that have continued to play a big role in American life then and today. Whatever America becomes will always be affected by those ancient squabbles. The governance of the nation by politicians of the two major political parties now in the United States (Republican and Democrat) has become central to what makes or mars the greatness of this unique country in the world. The people choose who will govern them and the people in government make the laws that govern the people who elected them. That arrangement is what defines what the country becomes for better or for worse. That affects the laws the people make in regulations that affect God in people's lives, the family unit, religious practices, rights and wrongs, life and death, black and white issues, peace and war at home and abroad and safe and unsafe streets within. It is that which we call politics that controls the affairs of the country and people.

The nineteen forties and fifties brought prosperity, satisfaction and peace in America. Americans were God and family oriented and happy. After World War 11, Americans who survived the war saw what was greater than them. Then the sixties threw a wrench that introduced drugs and youth indiscipline which altered the family structure. Since then, America has gradually been on the downward movement which is today more pronounced. From that downward trend to now, there have been "politically correct" attitudes and other socially unaccepted, brazen and blatant acts that are utterly un-American and anti-God in America.

The writer is looking at these issues. The Founding Fathers of the United States of America made a foundational declaration regarding the equality and rights of all people created by God. The Amendments to the Constitution laid the foundation for the nation pointing out inalienable rights to be enjoyed by all irrespective of one's status in life for peaceful coexistence and happiness for all. It established a political system which made those noble ideas functional for the people - noble ideas of happiness, prosperity and peace. How does politics advance or mar the success or otherwise of the Founding Fathers' vision? What kind of parents would one like to have if one was to choose – parents who will let one run wild and do whatever one wants or parents who would love one and train one to be the best (not the worst) one can be? What kind of a state or city would one like to live in – a responsibly managed, peaceful, well-ordered, crime free state and city or badly managed city or state, with no jobs but carefree, 'anything goes' State and City full of drug addicts, crimes and lawlessness? What kind of Governor, State and Federal legislators, City Council members would one like to run one's affairs? What kind of neighborhood would one like to live in and raise one's children to achieve the Pursuit of Happiness and the American Dream – crime, gang and drug infested neighborhood or sane and drug-free, gang-free, civilized and peaceful neighborhood? This writer looks in depth at those issues.

An everyday American would love to live in a prosperous and peaceful neighborhood, City, State and country for the pursuit of Happiness and the American Dream. Ordinarily parents choose States, Cities and neighborhoods conducive to raising their children. When neighborhoods become drug infested, parents start looking for other places to move to because children's education does not cohabit amicably with lawlessness. Usually, one of the competing issues must give up and the other takes over. Parents who have good values and money move out but the poor parents, even if they have the same values, cannot afford to leave the rundown neighborhoods. They are forced by circumstances to raise their children in crime-infested neighborhoods. That becomes the reality for those children - a reality that will become part of their life, which eventually impacts America just as it is now.

There is a standard agreement that a place becomes nice and livable when the people who govern the place are people who believe in the Creator and are people of good will, selfless, reasonable and competent managers of people and resources. If they are not, the place is run down and people are dissatisfied; those who are able to flee for a better place, will do so. This unfortunately is the situation in many cities and states managed by people of the same political party, policies and leaning in our country today.

The governments of States and Cities are run by the two political parties. Each of the main political parties has ideologies and policies that govern the party depending on the people who make up the party. Some ideologies are better than the others. That is why the laws and policies reflect the parties and the people in them. That too is the reason why one city runs better than the others based on who runs and makes the policies and laws that govern the people of a particular City or State. Those who respect life make laws that protect life both in the womb and outside the womb. These are generally called Conservatives while those who think they have the right to dispense of life at will are called Liberals or Progressives. The issue becomes: where do Liberals get the right to take life, which belongs only to God? The question of where this right comes from is at the center of the Pro and Against abortion debate, which has been under discussion in the last fifty plus years. Before 1973, American children in the womb were by and large safe and most of America was happy and peaceful with sizable and decent family structures. When the government devalues life, young gang bangers and some people take up arms and kill one another because either the court or government or both directly or indirectly say that it is fine to do so. Unfortunately, innocent lives are lost. But these are all our children.

Another divisive issue in the American political sphere is the gay and lesbian issue which has secretly been around since the sixties. The question about the morality of the same sex marriage has quietly been brewing in America for over forty years until the Supreme Court, which legalized abortion in 1973, also gave a green light for same sex marriage as a Constitutional right in 2015. Many Americans still think that same sex marriage is an aberration to human nature and God. An offshoot of gay lifestyle is transgenderism. With transgenderism a few people think they have the right to change the sex they were born with or that they can decide to be sexless even when they know that that concept could only exist in their mind. Transgenderism is part of LGBTQIA+ Community which is like a worm eating into the youngest of Americans in grade schools where they are being recruited into the community. This recruitment is the only way to maintain the community's existence, since neither two men nor two women can have a biological child. If an adult man wants to "become" a woman, that becomes his issue and problem between him and God, if he believes in God. But when the government of the United States of America empowers LGBTQIA+ community to teach, coerce and recruit unsuspecting children into the so-called alternative lifestyle, it is a lot of miles too far unacceptable.

When children are coerced into lifestyles that contradict their nature, they usually snap out of it when they become adults. But if they cannot go back to who and what they were before they were deceived, because of the nature of irreversible surgeries of transgenderism, their lives become a nightmare and unlivable. Lawlessness, depression and suicide become very preferrable options for them. Those who don't finalize their suicidal thoughts, lose interest in people, education and life in general. They become losers at an early age. A big number become criminals and homeless. Society and God become their enemies, and they become willful but miserable influencers for the devil. This is how some of our children have fallen prey to a life that goes nowhere.

Some members of the political class have dealt a wrong hand on the people who voted them into power. The courts and politicians are responsible for driving God out of schools; there are no religion or religious emblems in school while the gay colors decorate public schools, State Houses and of course, the People's House in Washington DC during so-called Pride Months. In God's place some people have now enthroned satanism, an unnatural lifestyle completely designed, implemented and supported by our government. When the power of government is used to support and enthrone evil as good, sin is glorified and from there on, anything goes. That seems to be where we are now. The way laws are crafted in some Mayoral districts, Cities and States, gives one an idea of who is in charge in those Cities and States. Where the criminal becomes the victim, one immediately knows who is running that City or Mayoral

District, Republicans or Democrats. It also tells one who the District Attorney and the Attorney General of the State is. But it is not accidental that drug addiction, crimes, homelessness, and degradation of life in States and Cities of America happen to be concentrated in those States and Cities run by the Democrat Party because their policies are the same. It is the same States and Cities experiencing mass exodus from them into Republican States and Cities to enjoy a better life with a reasonable cost of living. Despite this degeneration and failure of governance and leadership, the same failed politicians claim to be doing fine. That is how America lost objective truth and everything has become subjective. Truth has become whatever the individual says it is. Anybody in power can create their own reality and make laws to become anything they want them to be. This is precisely why LGBTQIA+ keeps the plus (+) at the end of their acronym because their "truth" changes all the time even though we know that truth is unchangeable. As it is now, no one knows where America is going at this point in her history. The only thing certain about the American movement is that it is going in the wrong direction. Immediate redemption, close to the Jesus Redemption, is needed to rescue the little good that is left.

CHAPTER ONE: BEFORE THINGS FELL OFF THE SHELF

The United States of America was globally known as a land of Freedom; a land of the brave, and above all, a land where the rest of the world likes to visit and copy from and in many cases stay. Many people within and without call America the beacon of hope; a city on the mountain for all to see. A shining example! When any part of the world needed help, it was the United States of America that stepped up to the call to help. Generally, America has a good heart. She is the most generous country in the whole world in giving financial help as well as the blood of her sons and daughters in wars to defend the cause of Freedom. That sounds fair. One of many such calls came during World War 11, when American Forces helped to liberate Europe in Normandy, France with the Allied Forces by ousting Nazi Germany. That liberation cost America a lot in money and personnel. That is an example of what America does.

When the war was raging in Europe, America remained neutral until Imperial Japan bombed Pearl Harbor without any reasonable provocation. Japan woke the sleeping giant. That Japanese assault, among other things, was the immediate reason America joined the Allied Forces in the Second World War. The United States of America went into the European theater of the war with all its might in personnel and her wealth. While the men were overseas fighting, the women were doing their own fighting at home. American women were mobilized to produce the weapons of war for the men fighting overseas. Women left the home to work in weapons factories for the first time. It is estimated that about 350,000 women served in the U. S. Army during World War 11, both at home and abroad. Between 1940 and 1945 the U.S. women force increased from 27 percent to 37 percent. During this time there was a recruiting effort to use a fictitious character "Rosie the Riveter" to attract more women to join the military as a patriotic gesture and it worked. Many American women joined the military. World War 11 opened the door for women to work outside the home and in varied types of jobs than before. The First Lady, Eleanor Roosevelt, through her husband, President Franklin D. Roosevelt and other women groups convinced General George Marshall to support the idea of introducing a women's service branch into the Army. It was ratified in May 1942 by Congress with the name "Women's Auxiliary Army Corps". Later it was upgraded to the "Women's Army Corps" with full military status.

With the men overseas fighting, American women had to balance working in the factories and taking care of the children as well. That combination of work and childcare created a problem of absenteeism at the factories. This problem was solved by the introduction of "The Lanham Act of 1940. This Act gave war related government grants for childcare services in communities where defense production was a major industry. Later in 1942 Eleanor Roosevelt urged her husband to pass the Community Factories Act, which led to the creation of the first United States government sponsored childcare center.

The American women, not only helped in the war effort, but they were also successful in raising the children at home. They did a fantastic job in raising the next generation who were respectful Americans who loved God, fellow citizens and country. Under this foundation built on respect for God, fellow citizens and country, the streets and people's property were safe. During this period America experienced hard work and valued the ethics of hard work. There was no room for laziness or handouts. Everybody saw hard work as a means to build good relationships based on respect, love and trust. It sharpened their sense of value for other people and their property. There was law and order in cities and neighborhoods across America. The tumult and destruction of the war of the forties in Europe and Japan paved the way for peace and a sense of humility in the United States and the world. The good old days!

THEN THE FIFTIES

When the second world war ended in 1945, surviving American soldiers came back home to their families after years of fighting in Europe and Asia. They reunited with their families and many of them started a new life. Teenage soldiers who went to war came back as responsible men ready to make something of themselves. Many of the American soldiers saw war and came close to death. They witnessed the deaths of their friends and people on both sides of the conflict. It was a humbling experience for many of them to be survivors and it showed in their lives afterwards. Perhaps that was why peace had a deeper meaning for them after those horrible experiences of war overseas. There was a big reunion and celebration for life by the returning soldiers and their families and friends at home. With the experience of war, a lot of people at home and overseas saw how fragile life was and how important family was as well. They had families to come back to. Many Americans did not return. The reality of the war was evident to both those who were in the war zones and those who were at home but heard the horror stories of war. Passing through war, hardship and the great depression gave many Americans a better sense and appreciation of life and all that it offered thereafter.

This period saw a tremendous number of American soldiers and non-soldiers get married. Returning soldiers proposed to and married the girl friends they left behind during the war. They had experienced something bigger than themselves. God had an even greater value and meaning to them than before. Life, country and family values became very important to American people. One could say that this period was a time when people experienced a religious awakening that brought them close to God. There was peace and harmony in families and American cities. This was primarily because after the war and the depression, most people had a very strong Faith in God and looked up to Him for guidance and protection. It was in this period that, on July 30th, 1956, Congress passed a law making "In God We Trust", the motto of the Nation. This proclamation was signed into law the same day by President Dwight Eisenhower. Since then, "In God We Trust" has appeared on all American currency notes and coins. This situation made the fifties one of the best times to live in America.

The economy was booming, and people had more money in their pockets than ever. There was a migration boom of people from all over the world. This created an unprecedented opportunity to experiment and utilize the talents of people migrating into the United States. All this innovation ushered in entrepreneurship and created a lot of jobs for everyone willing to work. People were ready for another and better life. Consequently, many households could afford to buy homes for the first time. It is estimated that about 13 million homes were built in the 1950s. That period witnessed what could be described as a perfect picture of the family consisting of hardworking parents with disciplined, respectful and law-abiding children. States, Cities and Counties were peaceful and beautiful. This period of American history is often referred to as "The Affluent Society of the 50s" because most of the people were well satisfied and happy. It is the period that produced hardworking, peaceful and happy people, who had great rapport with God as the engine driving the nation. Since there was respect and fear of God in people, there was mutual respect, and their property was also safe. People hardly locked their homes when they stepped out of the house.

While the men, the breadwinners, were in the fields and offices, most of the women stayed home to take care of the children, the next generation. Some of the women had part-time jobs however, as well as keeping the homes. It was also at this time that America witnessed the greatest number of children born in America. These children born approximately between 1946 and 1964 are generally referred to as the "Baby Boomers". During this time there was an abundance of food; people could afford homes and cars thereby enabling people to travel and enjoy a good network of newly built roads. Ownership of cars made it easy for people to enjoy the great outdoors and to eat out more often. This new development helped to popularize the fast-food experiment at the time. McDonald's restaurant, which specialized in hamburgers and milkshakes, blossomed in the fifties and never slowed down. In 1940 the McDonald brothers, Maurice (Mac) and Richard (Dick), founded McDonald's corporation, which revolutionized eating out in the fifties. Eating at McDonalds was a whole new and different experience of eating out. It spread like wildfire from San Bernardino, California to many parts of the United States.

A good number of families also had the privilege of owning a television set for the first time. After work people would relax and have fun in front of a television set. Radio and Television gave families the opportunity to have a good family down time with music and other shows. The popular music of post-World War 11 America was what was popularly described as "feel good" tunes. These were made popular by artists like Pat Boone, Rosemary Clooney, and Perry Como. On the other hand, there was another brand of music mainly popular among black Americans. We are talking about Blues and Jazz. In the post WW11 era, there were a lot of people movements and possibilities and experimentation all over America. For whatever reason, Blues, Jazz and Country music found a common ground in what became "Rock and Roll", a nightmare for parents of teenagers, who fell in love with it. For sure it was different and not too many parents were happy about its creation. It had the effect of desegregating white and black teens who were drawn to it. Rock and Roll of the fifties were made popular by artists like Elvis Presley, Chuck Berry, Little Richard, and the Crickets to name a few. Bringing people together, Rock and Roll liberalized dancing and brought out the unexpected and bizarre in teenagers. The lyrics were new and different. White middle and upper middle-class parents vehemently opposed their children mixing with other races and lower classes. This is how Dr. Steve Williams of the University of Southern Indiana described the white middle and upper middle class parents' sentiment about Rock and Roll:

"Suburban moms and dads are freaked out about their daughters hanging out with young black men listening to sexualized music".

Since the adult society frowned at this type of music, the young people loved and listened to it privately. To prove the parents right, sex and drugs and teen rebellion became byproducts of Rock and Roll. From liberating themselves from parents and adults, teenagers found a common cause in the liberation movement of the time. It became only natural for teenagers (black and white) to join hands with groups like the National Association for the Advancement of Colored People (NAACP) to fight for civil rights. Liberation and freedom from parents and segregated American society, was a common echo for both groups.

It was one of the best times to live in America on the one hand and the time of most discrimination between white and blacks on the other hand. The Civil Rights Act of 1954 was responsible for the desegregation of schools. By that act all American children were entitled to attend school anywhere they chose. Civil Rights groups had some victories through the courts. In the case "Brown vs Board of Education" the

Supreme Court overturned the policy of "separate but equal" because it violated equal protection under the law. Though this court ruling was not immediately and easily implemented, it was a good start on the road to equal opportunity for all. Elsewhere Rosa Parks and Rev. Martin Luther King, Jr. were making some inroads in dismantling segregation and inequality between whites and blacks especially in the South, where slavery was very strong. This period also saw some good things happening after people had witnessed the "Great Depression" firsthand.

The Fifties was also the time that launched America into prominence in aviation. The National Aeronautics and Space Administration (NASA) was born on October 1, 1958. After WW11, the cold war between the United States and the Soviet Union started. There was suspicion, competition and mistrust between the United States and the Soviet Union. Each side was trying to subvert and outdo the other in all aspects of life on earth and out of space. At the center of this strife was: which of the two nations would conquer Space first. There was an undeclared war on space. NASA was created in response to the Soviet Union's launch of SPUTNIK 1, its first satellite in orbit on October 4, 1957. This Soviet satellite launch came as a surprise to the United States of America and the world. Like a "pearl Harbor" moment, the United States was gingered into action. The launch of Sputnik by the Soviet Union woke the sleeping lion into action. On July 29, 1958, the United States Congress passed a legislation to establish NASA and it was signed into law by President Dwight Eisenhower. That kicked off the American "Space Race" which eventually put the first human beings on the moon on July 20, 1969. Three American Astronauts, Neal Armstrong, Buzz Aldrin and Mike Collins made America proud by doing what no human being had ever done before. While Astronaut Michael Collins was piloting the Space module, Neal Armstrong stepped on the moon while Buzz Aldrin took the first photographs before joining Neal Armstrong 19 minutes later the surface of the moon. Both men covered about 3,300 feet of walk on the moon, collecting moon soil and rocks, performing some scientific experiments and erected the American flag on the moon. This feat put the United States of America on a whole other place of prominence in the world. From that day on, every other nation has been trying to catch up with the United States in the race for the Universe.

CHAPTER TWO: THE SIXTIES AND THE DRUG AND SEX REVOLUTION

People got up one day, as it were, and things fell apart. The center could no longer hold. It is the arrival of the sixties. The "affluent society of the fifties"- conformity, peace, strong family units, economic prosperity and respect for God and others - was replaced by rebellion, chaos, non-conformity, less family values and general anarchy. The emergence of "The Hippies", which kicked off other similar groups, did not help the situation. For these young hippies, there was no objectivity, no protocol, no uniformity, no right, no wrong. It was all about **feelings**, the way you feel at any time is what counts. There was no dress code, no formality. This new movement was to challenge the 'status quo', authority, God and the establishment. They claimed they were disillusioned by some preceding events in their life. The assassination of President John F. Kenedy, Martin Luther King, Jr and Robert Kenedy seemed to have assassinated the hopes they had in those men and what they stood for. For them the violence of those assassinations was the beginning of violence and disorder in America. They were demoralized and thought that what their parents taught them about God, justice and all morality were perhaps not true if such good men could be assassinated. It appeared to them that those family values were not fair or just if their mentors could be killed like that. They decided to try something else. They were ready to venture into a totally new frontier. These young people put their own future into their own hands and were ready to try anything and experiment on anything and everything. The assassination of their hopes shook their faith in the moral principles they were taught. In a Voice of America (VOA) program "The Making of a Nation", Rick Kleinfeldt and Stan Busby captured the feelings of young people this way:

"A time of innocence and hope soon began to look like a time of anger and violence".

In other words, the innocence and hope of the fifties soon turned into loss of faith and hope, which were translated into the revolution, anger and violence of the sixties. Since the leaders of this movement were young men and women in desperation, their first line of attack was to challenge authority, family and God. Respect for God and "Honor your father and your mother" became obsolete beliefs of yester-years. Traditional marriage was no longer fashionable. "Free Sex" replaced family and marriage while cohabitation of unmarried young men and women became fashionable and a natural consequence of the movement's agenda and experimentation.

For every human action there is always a reaction and consequence. When these young adults chose this new path, there was an increase in student school dropouts as well as living away from home and parents. Since their code of conduct is "no boundaries", they had no qualms pushing into a new frontier of smoking, alcohol, dangerous drugs, free sex, out of wedlock pregnancies and unrestricted abortions, of course, to remove the responsibility of taking care of a child. Frequent rapes became the casualties of this lifestyle, where mind altering drugs were freely and frequently consumed. A lot of lives were lost among this group of young people through depression, suicide, drug-overdose and severe mental illness. This was the time when "homelessness", though new, had a nice ring to it because this group made it look normal and even desirable. Young men and women would voluntarily leave the comfort of a home to live in open-air communes, sometimes situated in bushes in the middle of nowhere without taking shower for days and weeks. Very bizarre!

The Vietnam War helped to worsen the situation because young people who were conscription doggers into the Military, found homes among the hippie communes. Of course, no recruitment officer would want a hippie-type person in the Military since lawlessness and indiscipline cannot coexist with military order, respect and discipline. These young Americans dogged conscription because of the way they dressed, looked and behaved. The bizarre became normal in "God's own country" of the United States of America for the first time. At this period, when war was raging in Vietnam, one could see a group of young, able-bodied, haggard looking young men and women pushing a car instead of riding in it just to make a statement, look antisocial and anti-establishment. No Military recruiter would go for people like that. And that precisely was what the hippies wanted.

It is always advisable to leave the gin in the bottle to keep the peace. But once 'the gin is out of the bottle', there is no going back. Since the launching of the sixties brand of philosophy, America has not been the same; worse still, the deterioration is getting worse by the year. To be fair to the sixties, there were some silver linings in that decade. One could call it the "Civil Rights" decade. It was also called the "we have had it with oppression" decade. The Black/White race issues and equality of human beings, granted by the First Amendment, were seriously confronted headlong for the first time and with a different approach - peaceful demonstration. Congress and the White house were forced by peaceful demonstrations to investigate the marginalization of the Black race and other minorities in America. One of the good results was the "Civil Rights Act" of 1967. That Congressional move opened up the way for the creation of Special Groups for protection. Different groups sought recognition through demonstration or rebellion.

We had the "Stonewall Rebellion" of June 28, 1969, in Greenwich village, New York. Many historians believe that the Stonewall Rebellion marked the official beginning of the gay rights movement in America. This lifestyle was going hand in hand with the hippie culture, which was anti-establishment and counterculture. Since the gay lifestyle was by its nature unnatural and anti-Christian, its acceptance did not get any real traction from the American people. But that did not stop the gay movement from pushing on. America was founded on Judeo Christian principles and homosexuality was condemned by God in both the Old and New Testaments of the Holy book. It was also condemned by the Muslim Holy Book, the Quran. The gay issue was not something the American people were ready to accept. Many States of the Federation passed laws prohibiting homosexual acts. They were called "Sodomy Laws" from the destruction of Sodom and Gomorrah in Genesis, Chapter 19. These laws were on the books until some politicians started to sympathize with the movement and passed laws favorable to the group based on their interpretation of the First Amendment and freedom. This political and later judicial involvement in the gay issues would later result in full acceptance of the movement where normal and established Christian culture and marriage were turned upside down to accommodate the gay movement. Eventually gay marriage would become legally acceptable in the United States of America on June 26, 2015, thanks to the sixties.

In the sixties the gay group rebranded itself and brought about new vocabulary to describe itself: They referred to themselves with words and expressions like "Freaks"; "Love children"; "Love In"; "Flower Children" and "Queer". For the hippie culture, what everyone regards as "abnormal" is 'normal'. Before now the belief in and worship of God, the marriage between a man and a woman, were normal and common practice in America and elsewhere. But non-religion, and lack of family responsibility, and not maintaining a home and family, are normal for the hippies and their gay associates. Certain behaviors that are natural and acceptable norms are not acceptable to this group merely because they want to be different and counterculture. Their philosophy is predicated on experimentation and trying out new things, natural or unnatural. Since these two groups see God from a different lens, their understanding of God, morality and experimentation were of course different.

Since the Hippies' religion and philosophy were experimentation and the consumption of mind-altering drugs, unorthodox substances would be quite for a change. Apart from Marijuana, the drug popularly known as "LSD", (hallucinating drug) was very common among these experimenting young men and women of the sixties. Consequently, there was no differentiation between men and women sometimes. The differentiation and function of the sexes all become blurred. The only important factor on their mind is that there is "one love"; we are all "love children "; we are "flower children " and we are "Queer" under LSD, of course. The introduction of the gay lifestyle got its footing in America in the sixties.

What is LSD? According to the Merriam-Webster dictionary, LSD stands for "Lysergic acid diethylamide" and is defined as "a semisynthetic organic $C_{20} H_{25} N_3 O$ derived from ergot that induces extreme sensory distortions, altered perceptions of reality, and intense emotional states, that may also produce delusions and paranoia, that may sometimes cause panic reactions in response to the effects experienced". LSD is sometimes called "acid". That definition tells the whole story of the effects this dangerous drug has on people. Is there any wonder who the consumers become after consumption?

When someone consumes something that would induce extreme sensory distortions of reality and alters the perceptions of reality and causes an intense emotional state, there is little, or no reality left in that person to operate rationally as a human. He or she is completely taken over by non-reality and confusion. When this situation becomes habitual, the individual's ability to recognize or differentiate a man from a woman becomes flawed. In that demented mind a man or a woman is all the same because the sense of reality is altered. The individual's state may also cause delusions or paranoia. Everything is seen through the prism of distortion of reality, and the individual wallows in the sphere of delusion and paranoia. Who would want his or her teacher, parents, friends, pilots, and maybe lawmakers to be in this state of mind? My guess is a full scale "Nobody" answer. We all would like the captain of the plane to be in sync with reality and not be given the liberty to make his/her own reality of what a Captain's reality should be while on duty.

It might be nice to know some of the key persons, who were behind this monstrosity of a drug that has had negatively far-reaching effects on not only America, but the entire world. One of the pioneers of LSD was a man called Augustus Owsley Stanley, the third. He was an underground Chemist based in California. Stanley manufactured several million doses of LSD, which he sold to an LSD advocate and Novelist called Ken Kesey, who was the main supplier of LSD to the musical group, "Grateful Dead ". Another notable major advocate of LSD was an American psychologist, Timothy Leary. These people facilitated the spread of LSD in New York East Village and San Francisco Haight-Ashbury neighborhoods, which were the two major centers of counterculture in the sixties in the United States of America. In the sixties Haight-Ashbury in San Francisco and New York East Village neighborhoods were like centers of pilgrimage for the Hippies. Young men and women from all over the country flocked these centers for a so-called 'religious' experience. Anywhere you see them, they stand out. The men started wearing long hair, stopped shaving their head and beard, having sex and doing drugs practically anywhere to defile their Judeo-Christian upbringing and erase America's prosperity, peace and age of innocence of the forties and fifties. Capitalism and working for a living would be against the hippie culture, which is counter establishment of which work is a part of. They desperately sought for another kind of spiritual meaning in life or at least have a good time in their newfound spirituality without religion. This sounds like communism in action. Does it surprise anyone that San Francisco and New York are the two LGBTQ+ biggest 'homes' in the United States then and now?

They reinvented a new way to ascend to and encounter God under the influence of LSD which they used as a way of seeking spiritual perfection. William J. Rorabaugh, an American Historian put it like this about the hippies' spirituality:

"The Hippie counterculture, more than anything else, was about LSD; seeking spiritual perfection through drugs, but particularly psychedelic drugs". "Hippies resent the societal pressure" he continued, "to conform to the "normal" standards of appearance, employment and lifestyle. By men wearing long hair and growing beards, taking drugs and exploring spirituality outside of the confines of the Judeo-Christian tradition, hippies sought to find more meaning in life or at least, have a good time".

The hippies were not political. The closest they would come to politics would be their association with Vietnam War doggers, who infiltrated their group. Naturally the hippies became anti-war participants in sympathy with the war doggers. But the Hippies had no interest in politics. After all, politics is part of the establishment, which they had vowed to dismantle. Professor Rorabough discussing their politics said: "Hippie politics was more a 'politics of no politics'. One of the things the Hippies said was 'you should do your own thing; you should do whatever you feel like doing'". That does not sound like politics at all. That was when they divorced objectivity and married subjectivity.

The Hippie subculture did adversely affect the young people of the 50s and 60s. But its influence seemed to have died as a movement in 1967; but its vestiges did not die. Steve Jobs and some other hippies assimilated into mainstream culture, according to Professor Rorabaugh. He also believed that Mr. Jobs embraced Buddhism after a trip to India in the early 70s. Later Steve Jobs conceived the idea of the personal computer as a way of putting computer power in the hands of ordinary people and taking it away from IBM, a big corporation and a part of the establishment. Though no longer externally a hippie in the original sense, Steve Jobs still had the philosophy of the Hippie subculture of dismantling the establishment. Professor Rorabaugh said this about him:

"Taking computer power away from giant corporations and giving it to ordinary people - what could be more anti-establishment than that?"

It appears that some hippies left the communes and dispersed to individually fight for the original philosophy. The so-called death of the hippie subculture was also facilitated by the end of the Vietnam war. At least nobody was running away from conscription anymore. Many of the hippies infiltrated into the mainstream population with their anticultural and experimentation with them. Some later became professors in universities and handed that subculture to their students who are alive and well today spreading that philosophy within and outside of American Universities. Silicon Valley absorbed some of them and their philosophy.

Before the sixties, American women were at home taking care of the future generation while the men went to acquire education, get a job to feed the family. This current family structure was questioned by the sixties. Women wanted to go to school and work outside the home as the men. This brewing idea was brought to prominence by Betty Friedan in a book she published called "The Feminine Mystique" in 1963. In her book, she urged women to wake up and take up roles hitherto played only by men. Because of her efforts, a series of laws were passed giving women equal rights as men. These laws were enforced through the help of activists and organizations like the "National Organization for Women" (NOW). The interplay of these innovations gave birth to what later became the Women's Liberation Movement. Only the future will show the wisdom or lack thereof of American women leaving the home for the workplace as it affects the Nation and the nation's children. The reality of all these is that women started to venture into unprotected areas of human endeavor. The gloves were off. Women commonly started to drink, smoke and do drugs like men and lost their innocence. Another bottle of gin lost its content; it could not be put back.

The Civil Rights movement continued to generate more and more movements leading to more protected classes and rights to a point of ridicule. America suddenly became conscious of different groups that would need emancipation or protected status. Civil rights movement started with black African Americans and stretched to other minorities like: Native Americans, Hispanics Americans, Emancipation of America Women and their ability to vote, and Disabled Americans. Later the protected classes included animals as endangered species and a protected class. As time went on, other groups wanted the force of law to back-up their group claim. Most prominent in this category would be the gay people and later the abortion rights activist groups. Over the years the gay culture (Gays and Lesbians) developed into a number of subgroups with the acronym that grew into the current- LGBTQIA+, each letter representing a subgroup.

Let us define and maybe analyze the representation of each letter for the sake of clarity.

Lesbian: A lesbian is a term used to describe a female, who is romantically and or sexually oriented toward the female gender. Put in another way, a lesbian is a female who is sexually attracted to another female.

Gay: Gay is a term used to refer to a homosexual person or the trait of being homosexual. "Homo" is Latin for "Man". Originally the word gay is a term that means "carefree"; "cheerful"; or "bright and showy". But now gay is primarily used to describe a man who is sexually attracted to another man.

Bisexual: This is a new terminology used to describe a person who experiences sexual, romantic, physical or spiritual attraction to more than one of the two genders - male and female.

Transgender: This is a term used to describe a person whose gender identity or physical gender does not correspond with the sex assigned at birth. He/she doesn't like the gender which nature assigns to him/her and does something to change it. This individual undergoes a medical procedure to produce his/her desired gender.

Queer: The term queer is defined as something differing in some way from what is usual or normal; it is something odd, strange or weird. Merriam-Webster dictionary defines current queer as something "of or relating to or characterized by sexual or romantic attraction to members of one's sex (the same sex attraction). It further describes queer as "to consider or interpret (something) from a perspective that rejects traditional categories of gender and sexuality or (outside the norms of natural sex activity). It characterizes a person who disregards the norms of human behavior.

Intersexual: This category new, refers to a group of people whose sexuality and sexual activity is not defined. It cuts across boundaries. There are no boundaries in their sexual operation. He or she cuts across the sexual spectrum of human behavior. In other words, the individual does not recognize the differentiation of the sexes.

Asexual or Aromantic or Agender or Ally: This group could be said to be anti sex, anti-romantic, but genderless. As "Ally" would suggest everything is everything.

Pangender: In the same way Pangender people would be those who believe that all people are one and united gender. In other words, there is no distinction among the sexes. It is all what you say; it is not what it is objectively but what this individual subjectively thinks it is.

Plus (+): This 'plus' category seems to suggest that there could be another or other sexual orientation groups that could spring up in the future. The group originally started as "Gays". Then it became "Gays and Lesbians". After that comes a group that are sexually attracted to both men and women - Bisexual and the list goes on. Since there is no limit to what a human may want, another group decided to re-create themselves, since God made a mistake in the first place. By going from being male to female or from female to male, through surgery, this group takes the name, transgender and the list goes on and on and on. That is perhaps why they decided to leave the door open by putting plus ("+") at the end. The question then becomes: At what point does the Federal government stop dishing out so-called protection status under the guise of civil rights and freedom?

CHAPTER THREE: HOW THE SEVENTIES, "THE 'ME' DECADE", AFFECTED AMERICA

The seventies were nicknamed "the me decade" by Tom Wolfe, a journalist. The sixties witnessed a period when people were more concerned with social and political justice issues. The rebellious youths of the sixties fighting the establishment, joined the civil rights groups to dismantle what they perceived as injustice in the system. But here comes the seventies where people's concerns shifted from social and political justice issues to individual's well-being. The emphasis was more selfish, so to speak. The fifties and part of the sixties were prosperous and affluent decades in America after World War11. The seventies saw a drastic change in the economy and politics of, not just America, but in the rest of the world. America had enjoyed a period of growth and prosperity after the end of World War 11. But all that changed when world events changed from good to bad. The price of oil and gas hit a new high due to the Arab oil embargo to the United States of America and Canada where oil was being rationed and people had to line up for days for gas. Many people left their cars in the filling stations overnight to retain their position when the station opened the next day. This affected the car industry in America which lost their competitive edge to Japanese automakers. The situation caused inflation making the price of goods and services to rise dramatically compared with people's earnings. A drop in energy affects everything, every commodity used by man (just as President Biden's war against fossil fuel has affected every commodity in the United States throughout his presidency). Naturally in the seventies people were forced to abandon social justice issues to embrace the survival of the self in harsh economic conditions.

A lot of Americans lost faith in politics itself. President J.F. Kennedy and Lyndon B. Johnson were the crusaders of the government for the good of the people of the sixties. But when the Nixon presidency ended in a disaster, many people lost hope in politics itself. Then came President Jimmy Carter's presidency. Though he was a good and upright man, who did not play Washington politics well; he was weak and ineffective as a president. He was seen by many as too soft to handle international affairs. Moreover, the Iranian hostage taking of Americans for 444 days under President Carter's watch, was the last blow to his presidency. During President Carter's presidency, a group of Iranian students stormed the American Embassy in Iran on November 4th, 1979, and took 66 Americans hostage because President Carter welcomed the ousted Shah of Iran into the United States for treatment. After releasing 14 hostages, (women, African Americans and a sick hostage) the students kept the remaining 52 hostages for 444 days before their release on January 21, 1981, a few hours after Republican President Reagan delivered his inaugural address. Apart from the poor economic conditions in America under Jimmy Carter, his hostage rescue effort in "Operation Eagle Claw" hit a brick wall. Several Helicopters used for the operation malfunctioned due to a severe desert sandstorm and the operation was aborted while the United States lost 8 servicemen. That further decreased American's faith in politics in general and President Carter in particular. For many Americans it was a turning point for everyone to look inward. It was like "to your tents, oh Israel", to quote from the Bible. The American people felt more comfortable taking care of themselves than the social justice and politics of the day.

The inward looking of the American people was exacerbated by the change of emphasis on the lifestyle of many of the baby boomers, who instead of going to college decided to get married and raise families. For them setting up their own families was more personal and relevant to them than marching on the streets for social justice issues. Many Americans became more helpful to themselves by being more inclined to enjoying music, reading self-help books which improve their lives and the comfort of a good home and good pastime in the home. Yes, the "me decade" is very appropriate for that decade. After the day's work many Americans sat as a family in front of a colored television to watch sports, comedies and detective stories. For some families it was listening or dancing to beautiful music. The Rock and Roll of the sixties were still relevant but new tunes and variations developed. The seventies produced

Punk Rock, the Wave and Heavy Metal. For this decade it was all about the self in music, fashion and sports to create fun for the individual. Self-consciousness of the seventies left a footprint on the decades that followed. In emphasizing the self, the "me decade" held on to some selfish tendencies of the sixties. Recall that the selfish and rebellious sixties introduced attitudes subjective in nature that fueled relativism and side kicked objective reality. The result of that subjective sentiment then is still reigning today in the media and the LGBTQIA+ community with a vengeance. The powerful media and the newly installed and equally powerful LGBTQIA+ community have unleashed their selfish ideology on the rest of America. Those who are not buying what the liberal left is selling are crushed by the weight of their power. Since the subjective views of the left are in the forefront, bad actors take advantage of the situation to project drugs, violence and lawlessness in the country for selfish purposes. America suddenly changed from harmless projection of the self in music, exercise and relaxation to a sinister subjective leftist ideology which is forcefully pushed on the rest of the nation. Well-meaning people mentally became hostages in their homes and country. They are no longer in control of their lives or families or neighborhood schools where their children go to learn. They are constantly living in fear of losing their lives or physical freedom. America changed and lost her equilibrium.

CHAPTER FOUR: HOMOSEXUALITY AND ITS TENDENCIES

What is homosexuality? Homosexuality is from a Latin word, 'Homo' which means "man" or human being in a generic sense. Some people believe that homosexuality comes from the Greek word 'homos' which means 'same' as in same sex. Homosexuality could be defined as "a romantic or sexual attraction or behavior between members of the same sex or gender". As a tendency it is a disorder in nature because nature has only two sexes or genders - male and female which are opposites that attract each other and makes animal and human species to reproduce. Without this opposite attraction arrangement of male and female, animals and human beings would have become extinct. That is why the idea of homosexuality is disordered. If everybody were to be homosexual, after the last generation, there would have been no more human beings on earth. Why would homosexuality be tenable? It would not make sense. For those who believe in God, why would God tell Adam (male) and Eve (female) to go and multiply and fill the earth. He could have created Adam (male) and Adomil (male) or Eve (female) and Evelyn (female) and mandated them to go and multiply and fill the earth. But He did not because the idea of man and man reproducing is incongruous.

Homosexuality is also unscientific. Human beings are made up of chromosomes X and Y. The female gender is made up of XX chromosomes and male gender is made up of XY chromosomes. It is as exact as science is. It is as constant as mathematics is constant. A man can produce either X or Y chromosomes, and a woman can only produce X chromosome. When a man produces a Y chromosome and it fuses with a woman's X chromosome, the child is male (XY). But when a man produces an X chromosome and it fuses with the woman's X chromosome, the child is female (XX). Only the man's chromosome determines the gender of a child since the woman can only produce X.

These have become as constant as science and mathematics; it is as one plus one is always two just as in the world of biological sciences, a man will always be a man, and a woman will always be a woman. We also know that opposites attract, male-female, positive-negative. To get electricity we need positive and negative energy. Doesn't that make gay attraction and the theory of transgenderism fictional? The idea of a man trans gendering into a woman is as utopian as it can be. It can only exist in the mind. Transgenderism is like what the Clown said in Shakespeare's "Twelfth Night", where the clown argues that:

Old English:

"Anything that's mended is but patcht:
Virtue that transgresses is but patcht with sin."

Modern English:
Anything that's mended is but patched:
Virtue that transgresses, is but patched with sin.)
(Twelfth Night, Act 1, Scene 5.)

Transgenderism is nothing but a patched job and not original. Consequently, it is unreal and utopian. Transgenderism does not exist in the world of realism.

God did not approve of either gay lifestyle or transgenderism in nature. And for those who believe in the Bible, the book of Genesis said that God made them male and female.

"God created man in his image, in the divine image he created him, male and female he created them. God blessed them, saying "Be fertile and multiply, fill the earth and subdue it…" (Genesis 1: 27-28)

The same is true in the animal world - male and female the purpose of procreation.

Also, God condemned and punished homosexuality outrightly in the Old Testament (Genesis Chapter 19:) and New Testament (Romans Chapter 1: 26 -27) 1 Cor. 6: 7-10) (1 Timothy Chapter 1: 9-10). Consequently, homosexuality is unnatural, anti-God and anti-science. How does religion view homosexuality? It is seen as a disorder that should be ordered and corrected through therapy like other disorders humans cause in nature because God does not make mistakes. On the other hand, Lucifer can and has been supplanting and disordering God's designs in creation from the time he was expelled from paradise because he does not want to be in error and in hell alone. As they say: "Evil likes company". This is the New Testament parable of the wheat and the weed. Jesus proposed a parable to his disciples:

"The kingdom of heaven may be likened to a man who sowed good seed in his field. While everyone was asleep his enemy came and sowed weeds all through the wheat and then went off. When the crop grew and bore fruit, the weeds appeared as well. The servants of the householder came to him and said, "Master, did you not sow good seed in your field? Where did the weeds come from? He answered them: "An enemy has done this...." (Matthew 13: 24-28). The devil has been fighting God since he was expelled from heaven.

The issue of homosexuality in the world is gaining as much momentum as people are losing momentum in their belief in, affiliation with and adherence to God. This is a serious trend that is spreading like wildfire in both churches and the wider society. The fuel that is sustaining this fire is Power, Selfishness and Materialism of the world. Remember that Lucifer tempted Jesus in the areas of power, selfishness and material things. If he did not spare Jesus, who is God, how do we think he will spare us? The devil is in the business of planting bad seeds in God's plantation. Lucifer is optimally using the instrument of Power, of Politicians and the Materialism in the world of atheist billionaires to promote bizarre groups like LGBTQIA+ to destabilize God's plan for mankind even in the church itself. There is nothing in LGBTQIA+ Community that promotes God. Nothing.

A few years ago, the Episcopal Church of America ordained the first gay bishop in the person of Bishop Gene Robinson, in 2003 as the Anglican bishop of New Hampshire. Gene Robinson divorced his wife in 1986 and married his boyfriend, Mark Andrew, two years after, in 1988. Gene Robinson's episcopal ordination was authorized with a 62 - 45 vote in the episcopal convention. That decision split the American Episcopal Church in two. Lucifer is doing a great job - sixty-two "yes" votes for his ordination and forty-five votes against his ordination. After that decision the opposing group formed the Anglican Church in North America

(ACNA). That same ordination also caused a rift in the greater Anglican Communion worldwide. Since then, there have been a lot more ordinations of openly gay priests and bishops in the Episcopal Church. Other churches, including the Catholic Church, have had openly and clandestine gay clergy in their fold as well. Lucifer is "no respecter of persons" as the saying goes. Individuals will answer the roll call when the time comes, not the Church as a group.

But a very relevant question should be: how can these dissidents in the Church explain to their congregations why God condemned homosexuality and destroyed whole cities of Sodom and Gomorrah in the Old Testament because of it? In chapter 19 of Genesis, the men of Sodom wanted to have sex with the two Angels, who disguised themselves as men on their way to destroy Sodom. The men of Sodom asked Lot:

"Where are the men who came to your house tonight? Bring them out to us so that we may have intimacies with them." (Gen. 19:5.)

Lot pleaded with them and said:

"I beg you, my brothers, not to do this wicked thing. I have two daughters who have never had intercourse with men. Let me bring them out to you, and you may do to them as you please. But don't do anything to these men, for you know they have come under the shelter of my roof." (Gen. 19: 6-8.)

They refused Lot's offer of his two daughters. When they wanted to force their way into Lot's house, the two angels blinded them with a bright light. The rest is history.

Sodom and Gomorrah were destroyed, sparing the family of Lot. How do gay bishops and clergy explain this to their congregation?

How do these Church leaders, who believe in, and practice homosexuality explain St. Paul's letter to the Romans to their congregations today? It reads:

"...Therefore, God handed them over to degrading passions. Their females exchanged natural relations for unnatural, and the males likewise gave up natural relations with females and burned with lust for one another. Males did shameful things with males and thus received in their own person the due penalty for their perversity..." (Romans Chapter 1: 26-27).

How do gay pastors in general explain Jesus' position on the issue of the sexes or genders in St. Mark's gospel? There, Jesus said:

"But from the beginning of creation, God made them male and female..." (Mark 10: 6) quoting from Genesis.

St. Matthew's gospel confirmed it when Jesus said:

"Have you not read that from the beginning the Creator made them male and female and said, "For this reason a man shall leave his father and mother and be joined to his wife, and the two shall become one flesh?" (Matthew. 19: 4)

All Christian clergy of different colors and persuasions profess Jesus Christ as their leader and mentor; they are called Christians because they are "Followers of Christ"; they all use the Bible as their authority to preach and to continue the gospel message in the world. How does a follower of Christ who uses the Bible to teach and profess something that contradicts Christ's teachings in the same Bible? A Minister of the Word cannot claim ignorance of the Word, which he professes to teach. Is it a matter of selfishness and human weakness on the part of the Minister? Or could it be a deliberate affront to God to make fun of God and religion? Lucifer's work! Are people deliberately planted in these churches by Lucifer's agents to be a constant reminder to the world about Lucifer's influence in the world? Many times, we see professed and unprofessed atheists playing significant roles in church and politics to dismantle God's kingdom on earth and lead people astray.

As they say, to influence decisions in an organization, one must be at the table. To reform or change the rules in any group, one must be in the group. Lucifer knows that too well. That is why he uses his position, power and wealth to influence issues to build his kingdom on earth. He goes into the leadership of the churches, who will then influence policies among the members of the churches. Lucifer takes advantage of the rich and the powerful in churches and political positions to advance his kingdom on earth. He has done it before and is still doing it again and again. As a high placed angel, he caused problems in Heaven and was kicked out of Heaven by God. For a while now the prince of darkness, especially since the sixties, has been using the revolution of the sixties in operating in different political arenas and churches in Europe and America with tremendous successes. One Church leader or one powerful political leader is by far more valuable to him than a host of ordinary individuals in church and politics. The expulsion of God in several American families and schools has been a huge success for the devil. This is done by a few political leaders and the effect becomes universal. If the devil gets the family, which is the foundation of humanity, he gets people in his camp. That is the grand plan. To implement the Grand Plan, the school is a "must" win to control the world because children are the future of mankind. What could be more ingenious on the part of the devil than that? The effect of that is that when many children are raised or been brought up in that godless atmosphere (family and school) lawlessness, drugs and sex become their god. Immorality, self-indulgence and aberration move from being casual and sinful things that happen to a few individuals, to becoming normal and second nature in people's lives. Sexual aberrations like LGBTQIA+ concept have become normal and generally acceptable in Europe and America especially. That is what is at stake and the goal of the gay community. How did we come to this?

Now that one frontier has been conquered in Europe and America, the prince of darkness has turned to the next frontier, Africa. Europe and America have conquered Africa before in various ways for centuries. We have had slavery and political conquest in Africa by Europe. The vulnerability of Africa has been exploited by Europe and America by offering loans and financial aid to Africa for a long time now. The most recent strategy is to transport European and American brands of morality to Africa as well. For a long time in the past, many African leaders were mere stooges to foreign powers because of the financial benefits those African leaders got for their individual families and friends. Like in slavery, those African leaders handed Africa to Europe and America for money. Based on that, European and more especially American politicians have come again to export LGBTQIA+ ethos and brand of morality into Africa as they have done with contraceptives since the eighties. But there seems to be a new brand of politicians in Africa now. For various reasons one of which is that many African leaders now are more educated and more convinced Christians, who have come to realize that "this place is not our home", according to Jim Reeves, the musician. They also seem to have understood that money is good; but it is not everything. They have realized too that after playing the game of politics in this world, the game of eternal life is a whole different ball game where partiality, money and power have no place. That is why many African leaders of today have refused to play the Lucifer game with homosexuality. Apart from Christianity, the current African leaders now realize that Africans have intrinsic cultures and customs that see homosexuality as unnatural and evil. They are not ready to play.

Regarding the position of African political leaders on homosexuality in Africa, Lucifer is working overtime to elicit help from different religious leaders all over the world to accomplish his goal because the failure or success of Christianity in the world seems to depend on Africa now. If we know that now, Lucifer has known it for a long time. But Ugandan political leaders, for example, have outrightly rejected homosexuality in its entirety and have passed a law, "Anti-Homosexual Act" (AHA) of 2014 against homosexuality with different levels of punishment, for different homosexual acts, graduated in years according to the offense. In Uganda, 96% of the people believe that "homosexuality is a way of life that should not be accepted by society." The strictest aspect of AHA stipulates that when an adult homosexual rapes or forces a minor or disabled people or transmitted terminal disease through homosexual acts, the punishment will be death. Some American politicians and some others have condemned this law in the strongest terms as being cruel. But look who's talking. American politicians? These American politicians seem to forget that America and some other western countries have condemned and put hundreds of people to death in the past and are still doing it. In America alone there are hundreds of death row inmates awaiting execution. It is okay when America condemns a criminal and puts him to death; but when Uganda passes a law that would do the same thing, it becomes cruel punishment. Let us look at the Uganda law again. If a homosexual man, for instance, rapes a minor or disabled man or child or transmitted a terminal disease through homosexual acts, (that means he has condemned the minor or disabled to death) and the government of Uganda condemns him to death and American politicians say it is cruel punishment. But that is what America does all the time. With a huge plank in their eyes, these American political leaders pretend to see well enough and attempt to remove the small spark in other countries' eyes ignoring the big plank in their own eyes. What an irony and hypocrisy! That resembles what John Kerry said in Nigeria when Nigeria passed a law against gay lifestyle. It was an international disgrace, a few years ago, when the then American Secretary of State, John Kerry, a Catholic, I might add, described the Nigerian law against homosexuality as "a setback". There you go again! It is remarkable that African leaders, Congresses and Parliaments have passed several laws prohibiting homosexuality in their countries. Bravo!

It has also been reported that some church leaders, including some in Africa, have joined in the condemnation of African leaders who have passed Anti-gay laws as Uganda did. The Churches which are against the government ban are American-led Christian groups. That, of course, is the American influence on those Christian Churches in Uganda and other African countries which are funded by some Churches from the United States of America. As they say: "he who pays the piper dictates the tune." Without the American money, those churches would not function. That is why they project their masters' voice. But there is a group in Uganda called the Inter-Religious Council of Uganda (IRCU) founded in 2001. This group has the membership of Catholic, Anglian and all the other Protestant religious groups, Bahai and Muslims etc. The IRCU group is in agreement with the government position on homosexual ban in the country. It would look disingenuous and awkward to see representatives of Jesus Christ eroding Jesus Christ's core principles. Who can really explain that to his congregation with a straight face?

As we observed earlier, Lucifer has made a considerable inroad into society via the gay culture in and outside the church especially in Europe and America. But at the same time, the majority of people in the world are still intact leading the opposition to this current societal decadence on the move. A very sizable number of churches worldwide are still "fighting the good fight" as St. Paul would say. Likewise on the political world stage, Lucifer has done a significant job in a number of leaders and countries in Europe and America. If this madness were restricted to Europe and America only, one could say, it is an American and European problem. But Lucifer would not stop in Europe and America. Christianity spreads to many other countries from the Middle East and then to the West. When Christianity came to Africa, she met deeply religious people fortified by their culture and customs. As a matter of fact, these African religions with their culture and customs made Christianity stronger and more stable in Africa because the people did not just accept a new religion but rather built on and updated what they already had. Surprise? Where did Christianity originate from? Africa! Countries of Africa were practicing paganism (worship of many deities, marrying many wives, sacrificing animals to God) as the Hebrews of the Old Testament were practicing at the instruction of the Hebrew God at the time, until the coming of Christ who came to fulfill all the prophecies of the Old Testament. Christ was the fulfillment of the Old Testament, and it did not take long before the Africans made the connection that Christianity was the fulfillment of the pagan religion, they had been practicing all the time. They not only accepted it, but they also cherished it. Today real Christianity is strong and vibrant in Africa because it was borne out of strong and enduring conviction. And you think that Lucifer doesn't know this? Remember he was the chief of the Angels before he was kicked out of Paradise. So not only does he know, but he also knows the weak link in Christianity and whom to use to expand his kingdom. This is how and why these countries in the West are being used to act as the agents of Lucifer in African countries without much success, at least for now. American politicians have been brandishing their wealth as a leverage to forcing African countries and leaders to accept abortion and more recently LGBTQIA+ culture to receive financial aid from the West. But recently in each case, they have woefully failed as far as abortion and homosexuality are concerned. African, as well as Muslim leaders and presidents have at least openly and legislatively rejected the idea that a man be allowed to marry another man, or a woman be allowed to marry another woman. Almost all these countries have passed laws prohibiting the legalization of LGBTQIA+ in their countries.

The last visit of the American Vice president, Kamala Harris, to three African countries with millions of dollar incentive did not yield any of President Joe Biden's desired result - to legitimize homosexuality in those three African countries to begin with. With one voice these African countries told Ms Harris that homosexuality was unnatural, against their customs and culture and therefore, un-African. To a country these leaders told President Biden that no amount of dollars will make them change their minds about their customary and cultural position on a matter fundamentally disordered, flawed and unnatural as LGBTQIA+. It is against African morals, customs and culture. These African leaders have made it clear to the West that colonization of Africa is no longer going to continue. The West has raped Africa for centuries and the current African leaders are no longer going to allow them to rape their morals, customs and culture, which they hold dearly.

As a result of African leaders' rejection of LGBTQIA+ in their countries, the Biden Administration has put sanctions; influenced World Bank restrictions in lending money to Uganda; issued business advisory, travel restrictions of Ugandan politicians to America; curtailing American aid to Uganda. The Biden administration wants to make an example of Uganda to scare other African countries. In a Press Gaggle by Deputy Press Secretary, Andrew Bates and NSC Coordinator for Strategic Communications, John Kirby En Route to Philadelphia, PA announced:

"As President Biden said, the enactment of Uganda Anti-Homosexual Act (AHA) is a tragic violation of human rights."

On December 4, 2023 United States Secretary of States, Anthony Blinken announced the expansion of the visa restriction policy to Uganda to "include current or former Uganda officials or others who are believed to be responsible for or complicit in, undermining the democratic process in Uganda or for policies or actions aimed at repressing members of marginalized or vulnerable populations." The Press Gaggle included "ending eligibility for the African Growth and Opportunity Act." It went on to say that "U.S Trade Representative informed the Government of Uganda that they will lose eligibility for the African Growth and Opportunity Act benefits on January 1, 2024 due to gross violations of internationally recognized human rights unless they publicly release an action plan for addressing human rights concerns and repeal the AHA."

This administration is using all its power to force Uganda and other African countries to accept homosexuality in Africa. That is really unfortunate.

CHAPTER FIVE: LGBTQIA+ AND ITS AGENDA IN THE USA

What is driving the LGBTQIA+ community in the United States of America? Why is this community forever adding to its acronym and ending with a plus at the end which seems to suggest that more subgroups are coming? That means there is a well-defined plan and expectation for more surprises. What is the goal and agenda of LGBTQIA+ in America? From our observation, some people in government, in politics and the leaders of the group seem to have an LGBTQIA+ grand plan for America. From the nature of the group its survival is at stake. The most crucial thing in their plan is how to keep the community alive as members age and die. They need young people to belong to their community, and they are doing everything to achieve this goal since the community is not naturally designed to multiply among themselves. Meanwhile the LGBTQIA+ community has acquired a lot of influence in the American government within a short period of time. They seem to have penetrated the corridors of power in the Local, State and Federal governments. How did they penetrate the Federal Government of the United States of America to an extent that they are shaping policies and calling the shots in key Departments in Biden's Administration like the Pentagon, Transportation, Education and Health and Human Services? Why did they get everything they wanted from the Federal Government as if the Government was on a spell? Only a few years ago, this group was asking to be recognized and accepted. But now they are running things and dragging and forcing the whole country to accept and believe in their culture. The group has so much power now that if one doesn't agree with their agenda, one is vilified, maligned and called homophobic because they now have an enormous power and can bankrupt or put one in prison. It is even worse than that. It is bad enough that a minority gay community in America is dominating most straight Americans; they now want to take over the children of America and make them members of the LGBTQIA+ family for survival. Survival instinct is a very powerful force. It is one thing for adults to choose to be gay or choose to transgender. But when children as young as twelve, thirteen and fourteen years old are drawn into becoming gays or hating the sex and pronouns they were born with, there is a big problem, America. This should be denounced by all Americans irrespective of their religion or politics.

Perhaps it was a bad idea to recognize gay culture in America. As they say: hindsight is 20/20 vision. Now that they have a seat at the table, they are trying very hard to take over the management of the house. How should we have treated the LGBTQIA+ condition and community? As human beings, we are all flawed, all sinful. There are some people who have drug addictions; some have alcohol addictions; some have sexual addictions or sexual identity addictions (sexual dysphoria); some have stealing addictions (kleptomaniacs) for whatever reasons. There are some men, who leave their beautiful wives at home and go after other women who pale in comparison to their wives. There are and have been some men and women who are attracted to people of their own sex. (Remember Sodom and Gomorrah thousands of years ago). These are all called addiction and abnormality. What do we do with addiction, sin or anomalies in nature? Should we accept and legalize them all or do we try to contain and manage them? Would it be for the good of society to legalize homicide, same sex marriage, stealing addiction, rape or adultery addictions because there are people in our society who are addicted to those behaviors? Maybe we should start to use our reasoning faculty once more.

From the beginning of humanity, these sins have always been there and will always be there. Before now we have always tried to contain them, not approve or recognize them. But with the recognition of gay lifestyle, we have crossed a forbidden line which has disrupted human and divine equilibrium. In the Old Testament God destroyed Sodom and Gomorrah to teach us to avoid homosexual behaviors. Whether we believe in God or not, we all should recognize at some level that homosexual actions are neither normal nor good for individuals or society. Irrespective of faith affiliations, human beings abhor the killing of another human being; they do not approve of people depriving others of their property, husband or wife by force or in secret; people everywhere abhor people testifying against their neighbor falsely, their peculiar situations or addictions notwithstanding. All over the world people do not pass laws to legalize stealing, homicide, rape and false testimony just to please some people in their community who are addicted to those crimes. It is not done. Why must homosexuality be different? Although these addictions are seen as evil, these anomalies still exist in our society today. We still see people angry, steal, rape, lie and kill. But we do not lobby or demonstrate to legalize those behaviors. We still have laws modeled after the Ten Commandments, to eradicate or at least, minimize them in our society. People of Faith call these anomalies, sins or flaws in human nature. Why do we choose to treat homosexuality differently to a point that we are now faced with dealing with the safety of our children encountering transgenderism in our schools? With reference to sins, people normally ask God to have mercy and forgive them; but with homosexuality, people, instead, choose to double down, recruit and promote it.

In our dealings with God, it is not that we sometimes fall short of expectation that offends God more; it is rather that we offend Him and stand to justify the offense by asking for human legislation to overrule God and legalize sin. It is even more offensive to God when we, not only offend God ourselves, but teach others to do the same. It gets even worse when we teach or introduce young, innocent people to take part in our shortcomings and addictions. It is called scandal and God hates scandals. As a nation we are enabling these forbidden behaviors. That is why Jesus said this concerning scandalizing young people:

"Whoever causes one of these little ones who believe in me to sin, it would be better for him to have a great millstone hung around his neck and to be drowned in the depth of the sea." (Matthew Chapter 18, Verse 6)

Introducing sin to children cries up to heaven for vengeance.

What should one do if one begins to have sex attraction to someone of the same sex? The answer to this is the same answer to: What should a married man do when he begins to have a sexual attraction to a woman who is not his wife? In both cases, the individuals should not entertain illicit sexual feelings in the two examples or feelings of rape or stealing or killing for that matter. The appropriate action would be to do what Alcoholic Anonymous (AA) teaches alcoholics to get sober and normal again. One must accept one's powerlessness and God's Almighty power to make changes in one's life. It requires humility and repentance, which means accepting God and the power of God to take over and heal the individual. One is better off staying away from the places and persons that trigger abnormal behaviors not enabling or defending them. Through therapy homosexuals have become normal and have had successful marriages with people of the opposite sex. There have been numerous testimonies to that effect. After all, the "B" in LGBTQIA+ means bisexual. That means that bisexuals have sex with both men and women. The progressives, some politicians and the media would persecute one for saying that a gay person can become normal through therapy because it would be "politically incorrect" as well as undercut the movement. Nobody wants to disprove the so-called "experts" who claim that gay lifestyle is natural and nothing can change it. Repentance, which is a turning around from the former position of sin and accepting Jesus/God, is the key to <u>any</u> disorder. Americans and people all over the world use the services of Therapists and Psychologists and Psychotherapists to get rid of addictions - sex addictions, alcohol addictions, drug addictions, same sex addictions etc. Our so-called "experts" belong to these groups, some of whom have had tremendous success in altering these abnormalities. This is not anything different. From the point of an individual surrender, Jesus takes over the healing process of the individual body and soul. But the individuals must acknowledge that they are weak and hopeless by their own power only and look up to Jesus for help. The problem people face today begins when one starts to justify the bad tendency, which is perverted and gathers people for demonstration for recognition by the government. These demonstrators want human recognition from courts and politicians. The courts, government and politicians who enable perverted and disordered behaviors are equally, if not more, culpable. Let no one deceive you to believing that <u>"something"</u> is lawful or legal according to Congress or the Judiciary, if that <u>"something"</u> is unlawful according to God's law, whether it be adultery, sinful cohabitation, homosexual acts or abortion. If God says it is wrong, it is forever wrong.

The recognition of gay culture in America has opened a lot of other issues that Americans must deal with in the years to come. The LGBTQIA+ community has a serious agenda. If gay lifestyle was not recognized by the courts and government, we would not be talking about the LGBTQIA+ agenda today; we wouldn't be worried about the safety of our children in school today; we wouldn't be worried about so many young people committing suicide after realizing that they have been deceived. The only way to explain the tragedy is that there is a grand plan to take over American society and ultimately the world to this new destination. When LGBTQIA+ is targeting the young people in grade schools across America through teaching and exposing under age children to sexual materials in the classroom and school libraries; when inviting drag queens, of all people, to read to children in our public schools and specifically introducing homosexual literature in school libraries, something is seriously wrong and points to a dangerous agenda. We are talking about underage children in grade and high schools. It is even a worse situation when the Federal government is part of the grand plan to enthrone LGBTQIA+ as a force in America with taxpayer money. That plan is nothing but a calculated plan to have a steady increase in the number of LGBTQIA+ people to have a commanding influence in American life and politics using other people's children and taxpayer money to achieve it.

Have you asked yourself why the LGBTQIA+ community has taken a stronghold in the White House starting from the presidency of President Barack Obama to President Biden? It is to transform America as President Obama told Americans years ago. President Barack Obama tactfully and permanently planted LGBTQIA+ community in the White House to start, continue and maintain the ascendency of the LGBTQIA+ power in the nation's seat of government during and after he had left office. He had a very soft spot for LGBTQIA+ community. Wasn't President Obama the first to appoint the greatest number of gays in the White House ever as well as the greatest number of gay Ambassadors in American history? That was part of what President Obama meant when he promised Americans that he was going to transform and change America. He is in the middle of this agenda. For sure, he has transformed America after eight years in office. President Joe Biden, who was President Obama's vice president, took over the mantle and even boasted of having the greatest number of LGBTQIA+ personnel in his cabinet and White House. He has surpassed his mentor, Barack Obama. This program was started under President Bill Clinton on a small scale. But it blossomed under Obama and now on steroids under President Biden even though he is not really in charge of the White House. He signed overpowers to the behind-the-scenes liberal electors who crowned him.

The gay community is visibly running the Biden White House with the personnel Obama left behind plus the new ones President Obama recommended to Biden from the background. We are talking about a cumulative twenty years of three presidents in the White House. President Obama is running the White House from his own house. In an article, Dan Avery wrote:

"Ruben Gonzales, vice president of LGBTQ Victory Institute, which trains advocates for queer candidates at all levels of government, noted that the LGBTQ people named to the incoming administration so far are all people of color". Mr. Avery reported that Gonzales' office, "has fielded more than 750 resumes, from those applying for cabinet-level posts to those seeking their first job in government", Ruben Gonzales told NBC News concerning getting LGBTQ+ staffers into Biden's administration roles. He continued:

"It began during the Clinton administration with David Mizner leveraging his influence to advocate for LGBTQ appointees, but it was really informal then".

For Gonzales, "An LGBTQ Cabinet appointment will ensure our community is part of decision-making at the highest levels," Gonzales said, "and would also be a lasting piece of Joe Biden's legacy on equality." This program, which started with President Clinton, "became more standardized during the Obama administration, which welcomed a record 330 out staffers, many assisted by the Presidential Appointment Initiative", Dan Avery wrote.

The LGBTQIA+ agenda is very clear to anyone whose eyes are open. The agenda is an openly aggressive take-over of America. What influence will the LGBTQIA+ have in the day to day running of the country? Certainly, President Obama understood this very well and had a robust LGBTQIA+ plan for America and the world too. It was not an accident that President Obama appointed about eight gay Ambassadors with a mandate to go out there and propagate the gay culture at their posts overseas. Remember that Ambassadors are the faces of the countries they represent in the host country. He wanted American gay Ambassadors to introduce the gay culture in those countries with financial bribes here and there. Though other recent presidents have appointed gay ambassadors, Presidents Obama and Biden hold the record.

When he went to his father's country, Kenya, President Obama tried to sell the LGBTQIA+ agenda to the people of Kenya. After his speech asking the Kenyan people to recognize and welcome gay lifestyle, it was his half-sister who immediately spoke after him and shut the idea down right there and she got the applause of the Kenyan people present in the audience. She let her half-brother know that the LGBTQIA+ thing is not an African thing. However, it was a big surprise to the Kenyans in the audience that the President of the number one country of the world did not see how ridiculous and unnatural the LGBTQIA+ idea was. To the people of Kenya and other African countries, it was rather disappointing that instead of giving financial aid to Africa for development, the Obama administration was exporting LGBTQ lifestyle just as the President Kennedy administration did, through the Rockefeller Foundation, exporting contraceptives and abortion to Africa as a form of aid. What do all these Presidents have in common? They are all Democrats. What a shame! Apparently, President Obama did not give them what they were expecting from him.

But President Biden, within four short years, has surpassed Obama in the support and promotion of LGBTQIA+ Community agenda in the United States of America and the world. It is not too surprising because President Biden, as President Obama's Vice president, was familiar with the blueprint of the plan to help LGBTQIA+ to take over America. Moreover, the inner workings of President Biden's administration have all the markings of the Obama's administration. Just recently President Biden appointed Jessica Stern, the Executive Director of an International LGBTQ+ Human Rights group, as his special envoy at the United States Department of State to promote and protect global LGBTQ+ rights with a salary of $180,000 taxpayer money. Her mandate is to protect and promote the gay agenda worldwide with our money.

Every year since President Joe Biden came into office, he has demonstrated to Americans that he is fully committed to promote LGBTQ+ agenda with a particular emphasis on Transgenderism. In his first year in office, barely three months he, on March 31, 2021, proclaimed March 31 as "Transgender Day 0f Visibility (TDOV). The President declared:

"Today, we honor and celebrate the achievements and resiliency of transgender individuals and communities", Biden said in the proclamation. "Transgender Day of Visibility (TDOV) recognizes the generations of struggle, activism and courage that have brought our country closer to full equality for transgender and gender non-binary people in the United States and around the world."

In 2024 March 31 was Easter Sunday, the day Christians all over the world celebrate the Resurrection of Jesus Christ. Despite that, President Biden, a proclaimed Catholic, still chose to proclaim:

"NOW, THEREFORE, I, Joseph R. Biden Jr, President of the United States of America, by virtue of the authority vested in me by the Constitution and the laws of the United States, do hereby proclaim March 31, 2024, as Transgender Day of Visibility," President Biden wrote in a Friday statement. "I call upon all Americans to join us in lifting up the lives and voices of transgender people throughout our nation and to work toward eliminating violence and discrimination based on gender identity."

This proclamation of "Transgender Day of Visibility" (TDOV) on Easter Sunday drew criticisms from many Americans irrespective of party or gender. One such critic was Caitlyn Jenner, an Olympic decathlete champion and reality TV star, who publicly came out as a transgender woman in 2015, took to **X**, formerly twitter, to slam Biden's message of support to transgender people, suggesting that he created TDOV to be held on the "most Holy of Holy days". She wrote:

"I am absolutely disgusted that Joe Biden has declared the most Holy of Holy days - a self-proclaimed devout Catholic - as transgender Day of Visibility. The only thing you should be declaring on this day is "He is Risen", she wrote.

In his proclamation President Biden was interested in calling on all Americans to join him in "lifting up the lives and voices of transgender people " and work towards "eliminating violence and discrimination based on gender identity". It is ironic that the President is not as much worried about the "uplifting of the lives" of so many poor Americans in the ghettos and homeless shelters nor is he concerned about "eliminating violence" in the poor neighborhoods of Chicago, Philadelphia, Baltimore, Fresno, Sacramento, Los Angeles, Oakland, San Francisco, Detroit, Seattle, Portland and of course Washington DC right in his neighborhood. These cities, unfortunately, are run by elected officials from his Party. Yes, he must protect those important to him, the Transgender Community when young, unemployed Americans are killing themselves every day on the streets of America. That is what happens when you give ALL POWER and AUTHORITY in your household to LGBTQIA+ people and are willing to sign everything they ask you to sign. The LGBTQIA+ members in the White House prepare the document and ask the President to sign and he signs it. Who blames them? The LGBTQIA+ community is looking after its interest especially when they have a good "rubber stamp" in the President.

When he boasted about appointing the greatest number of LGBTQIA+ community in his Cabinet and White House, President Biden was spot on. The Obama LGBTQIA+ plan is on track, entrenched and is well organized. Anise Parker, president of the "LGBTQ Victory Institute and LGBTQ Victory Fund" was right when she said:

"Members of Joe Biden's Cabinet will have tremendous influence over the policies and direction of the next administration, so it is essential an LGBTQ voice is at the table. Allies are invaluable but the impact of policies on LGBTQ lives is not always fully understood by someone outside our community."

Now it is working in Joe Biden's administration just as Ms. Parker said.

This ingenious community is planning. They have had eighteen years in and now they are planning for 'after the Biden administration', so that, according to Anise Parker, president of the LGBTQ Victory Institute and LGBTQ Victory Fund, "members of Joe Biden's Cabinet will have tremendous influence over the policies and direction of the next administration" after Joe Biden. That is why Anise Parker thinks "it is essential an LGBTQ voice is at the table" in Joe Biden's administration. It all happened as Parker wanted and predicted. The gay community has positioned itself well to take over America according to the plan. They have a "Victory Institute" and a "Victory Fund". The strategists are there, and the funds are there. Atheist George Soros and the George Soros of the world are ready and willing to make funds available to do what they must do to succeed in school boards, State and general elections, elections of District Attorneys to make sure their community's agenda are safeguarded. It has been documented that billionaire George Soros is a self-proclaimed Atheist. He doesn't care about morality or ethics in society and the good of the American people does not mean a thing for him, since he doesn't believe in God. In a December 20, 1998, CBS '60 Minutes' interview with Steve Croft, he openly said that he did not believe in God. Is there any wonder he supports politicians who want to plant LGBTQIA+ agenda and drive the notion of God as far as possible from the American society, especially from the next generation? One of the most strategic places the LGBTQIA+ people want to control is the education of the next generation. That is crucial for the grand plan and agenda. The LGBTQIA+ community has a strong foothold already in the Departments of Defense, Education, and Health and Human Services, thanks to President Biden's appointments. With those three Agencies, they can do a lot of damage to our children and the Military.

Just recently a man asked his wife to take their 7 year and 9-year-olds to their dentist. In the Dentist's office the dentist asked the children: "how do you want to be addressed, boy, girl or binary? The children were confused and did not know what the dentist was talking about. That was when their mother got upset and cut into the conversation. This has been the children's dentist for years. They are not new to the dentist. "So, what has changed since we were here last? " the mother asked the Dentist. The dentist was acting under the instruction of the department of Health and Human Services' directives regarding mandatory questions medical personnel must ask their school age patients. They are pushing transgender ideas to young children in schools and doctor's offices. And who is the Deputy Secretary of the Department of Health and Human Services? Dr. Rachael Levine, the transgender retired military doctor, is Biden's Deputy Secretary of Health and Human Services. Until her transgender surgery, she was Dr. Richard Levine, MD. There you go. They are coming for your children. The stupid question asked by the dentist was not his; it was the mandated question from the Department of Health and Human Services department to reinforce the pronoun idea planted in the students in school. This is Anise Parker's point of putting gay policies in place while they have the opportunity. Dr Levine and his group intend to plant the transgender idea in the children while they are young and impressionable. Sooner or later, it is expected that the children would be nursing the idea of switching their pronouns from 'he' to 'she' or 'binary' and perhaps changing gender. The Dentist would not ask an adult that stupid question because it was not meant for adults. That is how powerful and ingenious this group has become.

During the 2023 gay parade, the gay community brazenly came out and told America what their agenda has been all along. They have gotten enough power to speak out openly too. They are now comfortable to openly tell America what they are about. With a friendly administration and a solid and comfortable position in the White House and Cabinet appointments, they can now safely have a "second coming out". Why not? The gay community by its own volition and selfish end, has rejected procreation and having children. They know their community is in trouble if they don't recruit young people. They are smart enough to know that sooner or later their community would fizzle out if they don't have young people to increase and maintain their number somehow. Nature does not favor or support what is unnatural. Soon they will die off. So, they must do something on their own. To keep the gay community going, the LGBTQIA+ community must recruit new members from the straight community where there are children. That is why the community is doing everything possible to capture other people's children to keep their community alive. Smart but devious move! But the Biden administration does not either have enough sense to see what time it is, or they have sold their souls to the devil. None of these two options is good. The gay AGENDA was showcased during the 2023 gay parade across America. In broad daylight, in the view of hundreds of television cameras, there were groups of naked and half naked gay men, women and transgender people in LGBTQIA+ colors dancing in a parade on the street. What was the need to be naked in public if not to rub it in that the group is vicious and not of God? Is that the attitude of someone seeking acceptance into a decent society? I guess they are letting us know that the gin is out of the bottle already, and there's nothing anybody could do about it now. There was a particular group of naked men on bikes with a little girl on a bike too. The group of gay men and women were chanting:

"We're here;
we're queer;
we're not Gona stop;
we're coming for your children."

Let that echo sink in a little, America.
"We're here;
"we're queer;
"we're not gona stop;
"we're coming for your children."

That was bold and over the top, a sign that they are in charge. This is and has been the agenda all along: to make American children gays and lesbians and all the other incoherent and confusing categories in the acronym of their community. They have got the president and top cabinet officials in the administration dancing to their tune. There is no need to continue to be shy or hide the agenda and goal of the LGBTQIA+ Community anymore. This year they have made their "second coming out" of the agenda closet during the parade. Since they are convinced, there is no going back on the agenda and the operatives are in place with all the machinery in place, it is too late to stop the movement irrespective of who the next president after Biden is.

To top it off President Biden with his wife, Dr. Jill Biden showed their approval of this anomaly by hosting their own gay pride in the White House lawn. Without showing any respect to the President, the people's House and underage children in the audience, one of the lesbians or trans people in the parade removed her top clothes flashing her boobs to the public. Is this the best this group can produce - indecency even in front of children? Is that what the gay community is about? One can link this behavior to the indecent books and literature that show up in children's school libraries in the nation. This is what America has become under President Biden. It was later reported by the press Secretary, also a lesbian, that this individual lesbian or trans person, who exposed herself, has been banned from coming to the White House after that incident. Who will police that order since they run the place? Watch out, America; the predators are coming for your children. The LGBTQIA+ are no longer afraid of anybody because they have taken over the executive branch of government and they occupy key cabinet positions that relate to children. This is why they can openly tell the American parents to their faces, that they are "coming for your children." It is like telling parents that there is nothing they (parents) can do about it now. The agenda is working.

In his budget proposal to Congress, President Biden's Secretary of Defense, Lloyd Austin, is asking Congress to give DOD billions of dollars, millions of which will cover transgender surgeries for soldiers in the military. He wants taxpayers to foot the bill of men and women in the military, who go for elective transgender surgeries. When they went into the military, they had the genders assigned to them at birth, that is to say - nature. But now they want to override God and become something else at the expense of the American taxpayers. We did not think this madness had gone as far and bizarre as that. The Democrats in Congress have been pushing the appropriation of billions of dollars for this purpose. Thank God the Republicans hold the majority in the House and have held the line. Right now, the gay agenda is so watertight that even another president opposed to their plan would find it very difficult to undo because the plan had been in the works for a long time. The gin is already out of the bottle. At every step the entrenched LGBTQIA+ members would sabotage any efforts to dismantle some twenty plus years of their infiltration into the American system. While President Obama might not officially be in the White House right now, the Biden administration is Obama 2.0 - a third term. He was instrumental to most of the cabinet appointments and his influence for favors cannot be underrated.

President Joe Biden has willingly surrendered the nation's future to the LGBTQIA+ community with the likes of Randi Weingarten, the president of American Federation of Teachers Union, though he did not appoint her. She has enormous power among the teachers and the educational system in the country to get whatever her gay-lesbian community wants. President Weingarten controls the 1.6 million strong Teachers' Union and the teachers who teach our children. Why does LGBTQIA+ want to run our schools when they have no children, is the question Americans should be asking? The answer is that it fits into the plan, the blueprint of the agenda. The school is of course the place to catch the innocent, naive and unsuspecting children and turn as many as they can to alternative lifestyles, to plant the seed of anti-God, and mess up the heads of these children and give them a few years for the results to manifest in adulthood. Biden's Department of Justice (DOJ), and Federal Bureau of Investigation (FBI) are all in place to intimidate and harass any parents who try to interfere or stop this determined community to take over the lives of our children. They have told us that they are here, and they are queer. They have told us that they are not going to stop their invasion of the American family. They have told us that they are coming for our children. To realize their plan, they also need politicians that agree with them.

That is why they need people like Randi Weingarten, a Democrat and lesbian, married to Sharon Kleinbaum, another lesbian. Randi controls 135.1 million dollars of the American Federation of Teachers Union. Where do you think her allegiance has been all these years? Where do you think her allegiance will be now that Dr. Rachel Levine oversees the Department of Health and Human Services as the Deputy Secretary? After all, they belong to the same community. To show where her allegiance is, her Teachers' Union donated 45.8 million dollars to the Democrats (98%) and only 682 thousand dollars to Republicans (1%). Not up to 1 million dollars against 45.8 million dollars to Democrats! Don't you see that there is no accident in LGBTQIA+ plans vis a vis who they want in the White House and other elective positions of government. It highlights what is taught in schools these days about how cool they think it is for grade school children to become gay and transgender children.

It was just a few short years ago that the Obama administration introduced unisex restrooms in grade schools to accommodate minority gay students in grade schools. A so-called transgender girl could go into a real female restroom in our public schools. Unfortunately, the Biden administration has doubled down on this ridiculous policy even though there have been cases of so-called transgender 'girls' sexually assaulting biological female students in school restrooms. In each case the school administrators covered the assaults and transferred the perpetrators to other schools around. The gay community is running the show, after all. In, at least one case, there was a repeat of the sexual assault in the new school where the perpetrator was posted. Of course, there was no repercussion because of the powers that run the system. President Obama had foresight, and it is working as he wanted it.

This trans madness has also appeared in the prison system in a lot of States in America. A transgender "girl" in a female prison has impregnated two females in the prison. In an article published by Tat Bellamy-Walker July 19, 2022, Tat Bellamy-Walker reported:

"A transgender inmate has been transferred out of the only women's prison in New Jersey after impregnating two female inmates." The article continued: "Demi Minor, 27, (the inmate) has been moved to the vulnerable housing Unit at the Garden State Youth Correctional Facility, a prison for young adults ages 18 to 30, according to Dan Sperrazza, a New Jersey Department of Corrections spokesman."

The housing of men and women in the same unit in this case was because of a settlement between the New Jersey Department of Corrections and New Jersey ACLU, which took them to court resulting in housing the likes of inmate Demi Minor with female inmates. ACLU, of course, is as left as left can be and doesn't care. Yes, this trans lie will continue to be sold if the Biden government and ACLU are pedaling it. Demi Minor is a man who says he is a woman and is housed with women. There you go. A man will always be a man no matter what the transgender community says. A female cannot impregnate another female. Period. Everybody knows that; but it is not "politically correct" to admit that this whole transgender thing is a lie. This is what happens when people deliberately choose to live lives of "lies" that a man can become a woman just because he said so.

Can anyone forget how transgender girls and women have hijacked girls and women sports under this same administration? That, in effect, has nullified "Title Nine" which recognized that girls and women belonged to a different category of sports from boys' and men's sports. Now men have dominated Female Sports since men in female clothes are winning and taking home all the gold and University Scholarships in colleges in the United States. The women have gone back to the status quo. Right now, Women in College Sports have no place in Female Sports anymore. All that any man needs to do to get into Female Sports in college is to declare that he is a transgender woman and she is in. With 'her' masculine muscle and physique 'she' will become the champion of whichever sport 'she' plays in. 'She' could have been a mediocre player in his area of sports as a man. But as a transgender woman competing with women, she becomes a champion all the time, thanks to the trans agenda and the Biden administration. When the women in college sports complained against this recent practice, the administration and the media called them "transphobic" as always. A well-meaning administration would have created another category or association as was done when we had only two genders in Basketball, for instance. In American Basketball we have the Men's Basketball Association and Women's Basketball Association. Since the government has created other genders to satisfy the gay community, why not create two more categories for the transgender people. They could have one transgender man and another as transgender women Basketball or Swimming Associations. As it stands now the Biden administration and the gay community are not willing to do that, which seems to suggest that the goal from the beginning was to cheat the ladies.

As of now President Obama's LGBTQIA+ plan is working as planned by him and his fellow Democrats and the president who succeeded him. Grade school gay recruits are in progress and students have been subliminally coerced and encouraged to have sex changes without parental consent or knowledge. Parents are now the last to know that their children have undergone sex change. That is how to maintain the Community. The Biden administration has given grade school children, who even now, are not allowed to drive or drink alcohol, the right to make a permanent and long-lasting decision of sex change without the knowledge of their parents. When teens get their driving "learner's permit", they cannot legally go to practice on their own without the instructor or one of their parents or an approved adult in the car. I guess every rule must be broken to appease the gay community which wants to recruit our children into their community at all costs with the help of the President's appointees. Already President Biden and his LGBTQIA+ high Cabinet officers have made plans to "help" these children to transition into whatever they want them to transition into. They have the Defense Department, Education Department and the

Health and Human Services Department tightly secured with able hands like the transgender deputy Secretary of Health and Human Services in the person of retired Admiral Dr. Rachel Levine, MD., Undersecretary of Defense in the person of Shawn Skelly and the President of the American Federation Teachers Union, Randi Weingarten controlling the teachers of America. The disastrous effects of Obama and Biden presidencies will be far-reaching in years to come.

It used to be that children were advised that if a person gives them a command or an instruction to do something and tells them not to let their parents know, they were advised to run as far as their legs could carry them from such a person. But in President Biden's administration children have been instructed not to let their parents know about their sex change plan until after surgery. What does that tell you about how sinister this exercise of transgenderism is? The tragic aftermath is that school administrations would tell parents to give their children "gender affirming care" after the fact and threaten to take the children away from them if they don't. Which America is this? Is this China, North Korea, Russia or Iran? "Gender affirming care" meaning that parents are forced to go along with encouraging the action of sex change they had no knowledge of and do not believe in or else their children would be taken away from them? What a callous and mental torture to parents! That is mental abuse to parents. But to whom will parents go to complain about this abuse? Nobody but the perpetrators! Not even in a communist country! These are children as young as 12 years. This administration has allowed adults in positions of power to use that power to mutilate 12-year-olds and give them hormone pills and puberty blockers and rob innocent and unsuspecting children of a normal life to appease the Gay Community and perpetuate the gay agenda in America. Unfortunately, the enabling politicians know very well that these children will eventually, at about age twenty-five, find out that their lives have been ruined by adults, who were supposed to take care of them. These callous actors also know that many of these children will commit suicide eventually when they discover that they could neither function as males nor as females after the so-called sex change. Adults, who were supposed to protect them, have betrayed and deceived them and robbed them of their youth and innocence. That is a classic definition of rape - rape of innocent children by their politicians and government.

Except the parents and unfortunately the deceived children, all the other actors in this unfortunate drama would go home at the end of the day feeling happy that they have won a political point or that they have increased their chances of perpetuating and propagating their community's lifestyle in America. That is all that matters to them; to ruin the lives of other people's children means nothing to them. For these perpetrators, the tragedy experienced in millions of American families, becomes a joyful realization of the grand plan they have had for the country. It also guarantees the winning of a few more elections or reelections for the politicians with hands stained in the blood of the innocent children. This sinister agenda is the only way to keep the gay culture alive since neither two men nor two women can reproduce to keep their gay fantasy alive. The architects of this utopia know that if all the gay community was put in an enclosed city of their choice with nobody going in or out, that community would become extinct after about fifty years when everyone in that community would be dead. That is their fear, and our enabling government is helping them to use our children as their guinea pigs to continue to live in this utopian bubble.

Where exactly is the "Left" taking America? Today we know that America is in shambles: people are unsafe in their homes, unsafe on the streets; there is violence everywhere, youth drug epidemics, high teen suicide rate, low birth rate, killing of innocent babies in the womb and extreme hopelessness and homelessness at every corner of the United States these past few years. Unfortunately, those responsible for the malaise are doubling down on their actions. What will America look like in the next twenty years? Why does this administration use its energy and resources on alternate lifestyles instead of fixing the drug epidemics, crime and homelessness in the country? It is probably because the LGBTQIA+ people are running the White House, and they must table their own issues first. But why are the American people willing to accommodate people living in this falsehood, deception and hypocrisy?

Talking about deception and hypocrisy, Biden's transgender Deputy Secretary of Health and Human Services Department, Dr. Rachel Devine, has been the mouthpiece and defender of minor transgenderism and of hormone pills and puberty blockers for minors. But when she was asked why she waited till she was forty years as a man before transitioning into a woman and why she is now advocating transgender surgeries for teens, she said:

"My transition was very different because …I transitioned over 10 years," saying she never really considered it until in her 40s when it "became more in the culture." She added: "I have no regrets because if I had transitioned when I was young then I wouldn't have my children. I can't imagine a life without my children." she said of Dayna (daughter) and David (son), both now adults. The truth is now out, America.

There you have it, America. Dr. Rachel Levine enjoys having children; but she is very anxious and desperate to cut off the breasts and genitals of minor children, other people's children and deprive them of the right to have their own children. The truth at last! She says she cannot imagine a life without her children, but she is willing to permanently and perpetually deprive other people's children of having and enjoying their own children. If that is not criminal, tell me what is.

According to Reuters Dr. Levine claims that treatments like hormone and puberty blockers are "medically necessary, safe and effective" and crucial for trans youth suffering depression and "attempting suicide at an alarming rate." Defending her actions she said: "Gender-affirming care is medical care. Gender-affirming care is mental care. And gender-affirming care is suicide prevention care," and she vows to "try everything we can legally" to block states from implementing laws blocking treatments. Yes, she is the top brass in Health and Human Services in the country. She will fight to have her way, thanks to our president who put her there. For Dr. Levine puberty blockers and hormone pills are safe and cool for minors. But the National Health Service (NHS) of the United Kingdom disagrees. On March 13, 2024, the NHS banned puberty blockers for transgender minors questioning its safety for children. While countries like the UK are banning hormone pills and puberty blockers for minors, the United States of America is doubling down on them because a member of the LGBTQIA+ community is in charge. This is what happens when you let the cat oversee the hen house. According to Dr. Levine hormone pills and puberty blockers are "medically necessary, safe and effective and crucial for trans youth suffering depression and "attempting suicide…" But why are they depressed and suicidal, one may ask? In a lot of ways these medications are like "medicine after death". After mutilation of children Dr. Levine prescribes medication to stop children from suicide and depression caused by Dr. Levine and her community. Bravo, Doc! They have been put through an unnecessary procedure that is irreversible and then given medication. To what avail? Yet our government is sleeping on the wheels while that is happening.

The erosion of morality and commonsense in our public schools has gradually become an American culture with LBGTQIA+ community in charge. Like all cultures, they seem to have some permanence. The authorities have selected and posted LGBTQIA+ counselors and some teachers to indoctrinate children about how to transition into genders other than what they are by nature. The government or someone in government has always been an enabler in these efforts to promote gender surgeries in hospitals. An article in Washington Free Beacon revealed that it has uncovered the "coordination between more than 2200 health systems in the U.S. and Human Rights Campaign" (HRC), the nation's largest LGBTQ's lobbying Organization regarding radical gender ideology in the healthcare system to downplay restrictions on gender surgeries on minors. To protect the employees in the system, Senator Marco Rubio (R-FL) has introduced a bill in the senate, co-sponsored by Senator JD Vance (R-OH), Senator Cindy Hyde-Smith (R-MS) and Senator Thom Tillis (R-NC) to stop all hospitals taking Federal money from participating in such dubious LGBTQ's maneuvers. "It is deeply disturbing to see the progressive left infiltrate the American healthcare system and compromise the quality of patient care in the process. I am introducing the Protecting Conscience in Healthcare Act to stop this harmful, radical gender ideology in American hospitals and healthcare facilities", Rubio said. And where do you think that Bill is going with Chuck Shumer, (D-NY) as the Leader of the Senate? It is dead on arrival, of course. The LGBTQIA+ community has been under the radar setting things up for the good of their community for a long time now. There have been so many things going on under the radar since the eight years of the Obama administration. It is thanks to Covid 19 lockdown that some of these dubious schemes came to light. It was also at that time that parents shockingly found out what their children had been exposed to in public schools. Before that discovery, parents trusted teachers and school administrators with their children and dropped them off every morning thinking that their children were learning the traditional subjects, not knowing that their children were being indoctrinated into becoming LGBTQIA+ members. The indecent exposure to children in public schools has been going on for a long time before Covid 19. This has been the agenda and part of what is wrong with America today.

That discovery led to many more parents going to school board meetings to confront their elected board members. It has been revealed that these elected members were not happy to see parents get involved in the education of their children. Parents wanted to know why gay and pornographic materials were displayed in the classrooms and school libraries for underage children. They wanted to know why teachers and administration were indoctrinating their children with LGBTQIA+ materials in the library. Ordinarily this revelation would have resulted in the Department of Education investigating the matter and dealing with such school boards and ending the ridiculous indoctrination and bringing back sanity in the school system. But that was not what happened. To show that their actions came from above, the school boards and the school administrations, through the Department of Education, appealed to President Biden, who unleashed the powers of the Department of Justice (DOJ) and Federal Bureau of Investigation (FBI) to intimidate and arrest some parents. The parents were described by the DOJ as "domestic terrorists" just because the parents wanted to know why their minors were exposed to gay literature. Talking about giving a dog a bad name to kill it! Parents were called "Domestic terrorists" because they were trying to get involved in the education of their children? This is what America has become. Since the gay community is all over the White House and High Cabinet positions that can reach the President's ear, the President used the power and the tools of intimidation to scare and arrest some parents. How did America get here, we ask? Have we come to a place in our country where children cannot be allowed to be children any longer? Have we come to a place in America where parents have no right to get involved in the education of their children because this administration has handed over the education of their children into the hands of the LGBTQIA+ community which chose not to have children of their own? The people who oversee raising American children have "no horse in the race"; and they should have no stake in the education of children. What is the interest of the LGBTQIA+ Community <u>desperately</u> wanting to oversee educating children when they have none? And the government agrees with them and allows them to display their literature in public school libraries. Let us flip the picture. What if the LGBTQIA+ community were an Episcopalian or Catholic or Muslim subgroup? What would have happened if a Catholic or Muslim teacher or administrator had put Catholic or Muslim magazines, literature or doctrinal books in the public-school library and some parents objected to the presence of such materials? Would President Biden have unleashed the DOJ and FBI on the parents who objected to Episcopalian or Catholic or Muslim materials displayed in a public-school library? Even then, that would have been just doctrinal literature, not pornography to underage children. But I will let you answer the question. Would he do that?

The Biden administration has turned life upside down in many respects to accommodate this one community. Before now a teacher was not allowed to administer aspirin to a sick child in school without the consent of the parents. Before now, a sixteen- or seventeen-year-old boy or girl's consent in a consensual sex with an adult in school was and still is a statutory rape because he or she could not, by law make such a decision at age sixteen or seventeen. But under this administration a twelve-year-old can "make" a decision to change his or her gender, a change that has far reaching consequences than administering aspirin to a child in school, without the consent of one of the parents. Before now it was illegal and still is for a group of children, even on their own, to assemble and say prayers in a public school. There is still a standing policy that prohibits students from wearing clothes that have any words or inscriptions pertaining to God or religion to a public school. But in Biden's administration, students were allowed to wear LGBTQIA+ colors to school during "pride" month without any repercussions. Even in some school's students were encouraged by the school administration to come to school with clothes that have LGBTQAI+ colors, slogans and "pride" propaganda during 'gay pride month' as a form of solidarity with gay students.

At the same time there has never been a time Pentecostal or other Christian students have been allowed to wear images of Christ or the Cross or images of Mary or Christian Bible quotes against abortion to any public school. That would never happen in a public school. Whereas it was and still is not allowed for staff to administer any form of medication to students in school without the permission of one of the parents, in Biden's America, teachers encourage minors and even drive them to abortion clinics and places of sex change during school hours. Now it is 'gender affirmation' when school counselors and teachers in public schools educate and encourage their students to change their gender without the permission of their parents. It is the same tactics that abortion proponents used and still use to glamorize abortion by calling it "women's healthcare services". Helping a woman to kill the baby in her womb has become "women's healthcare services" just as helping and encouraging children to transition into another sex is "gender affirmation". These counselors and teachers, some of whom belong to the gay community, do these things boldly because they have a very strong support and backing in the White House, DOJ, FBI, Departments of Education and Health and Human Services, which have LGBTQAI+ members in very high positions of power. Some teachers and administrators who have moral objection to these unwholesome actions, end up going along with them because of the punitive and vindictive measures they would have to face if they don't comply with the policy of Biden's administration. The DOJ and FBI are ready to pounce on any such dissenters. It would be foolhardy for such teachers and administrators to be in front of Biden's fast freight train by running counter to the administration and jeopardize the only source of their family livelihood. They had to put food on the table, pay their house rent etc. They would not dare an administration that will go to any length to use the Federal Government machinery to crush anyone who does not comply with the mandates of the administration.

It should be made clear here that transgender surgeries on minors are permanent mutilations of breasts, ovaries and genitals on unsuspecting minors who don't really know what they want at that age. Some adult Americans have the nerves to do that to American minors and don't care what happens in their lives ten, fifteen years down the line. Does anybody care if such victims become depressed, homeless, alcoholics, drug addicts the rest of their lives or even commit suicide when they realize what happened to them? We already know that there is a high rate of suicide among teens in the last few decades. Even though teen and youth suicide are high already, researchers have found that suicide among lesbian, gay, bisexual, and transgender (LGBT) youth are comparatively higher than among the general population. LGBTQ+ teens and young adults have one of the highest rates of suicide attempts in the US and elsewhere. According to a CNN report,

"People who identify as transgender have significantly higher rates of suicide and suicide attempts compared with the rest of the population, according to a population-level study out of Denmark." It went on to say: "The study of more than 6.6 million people found that those who identified as trans had 7.7 times the rate of suicide attempts and 3.5 times the rate of suicide deaths than the broader Danish population." In the United States, CNN reported a similar statistic:

"Recent studies in the US show that 82% of people who identify as transgender said they considered killing themselves, and 40% have attempted suicide, with the highest numbers of suicides among trans youth. The Trevor Project's 2023 US National Survey on the Mental Health of LGBTQ Young People found that over half of trans or binary youth had seriously considered attempting suicide in the previous year." It added that "about 20% had attempted suicide in the previous year and about 3 in 5 transgender or nonbinary youth who wanted access to care were unable to get it."

Do our politicians see these statistics? Our youths have been confused and messed up by drugs that push some of them to commit suicide. Yet some of our elected officials add transgenderism to the same young people's minds. Why do transgender youths commit or attempt to commit suicide? Some transgender supporters seem to suggest that it is because they don't get "affirmation" from the public. That might be a tiny reason for suicide. Many adults understand and accept to go through with a procedure like transgender, and they do not care about who does or doesn't affirm them. The crux of the matter is: these are children who do not know what they are doing. They follow the direction and advice of adults placed in charge of them and they trust them completely. But why do people not affirm them anyway? It is because transgenderism is not considered natural or proper to many Americans. So, anyone pushing children for transgender surgery should not expect the whole world to go along with them before or after. They should check their "ego" and "selfishness" at the door before they go into this unpredictable venture. Mature adults who go through transgender surgery, do not look for sympathizers or affirmation because they have made an adult decision and are ready to live with it no matter what comes up. We cannot say the same thing about teens who are being deceived and indoctrinated by the LGBTQ community with the cooperation of some elected politicians to embark on a venture they did not understand. When 82 percent of transgender youths have considered and 40% have attempted suicide, there is a very big problem with recruiting teens to go through this dangerous exercise. That problem does not rest on other people who don't affirm, but on the trans youths and their enablers.

The ordinary preoccupation of students and young people everywhere in the world has been and should be about their studies in preparation for a career they would like to pursue in life to become somebody someday. This time in a youth's life is the time of aspiration for the future. It is a time for growing and having a good time, not a time of confusion, disillusionment, or a time to think about suicide. But instead, the Obama and Biden administrations have enthroned and endowed the gay adult community of America with power to confuse, recruit and coerce underage children in grade schools in America to an "alternate lifestyle", which is flawed and unnatural. Teens are not equipped to worry about such issues as gender pronouns and transgender issues at that age. But what is the consequence of that "brilliant" idea by our presidents and democrats? Suicide and suicide attempt among teens and young adults who abandon their education and must concentrate on the monster they have been made to become and cannot live with it! And somebody is calling on parents and others to "affirm" them when the damage is done without their knowledge. Affirmation from heaven will not undo the damage; the mutilated body is permanent and cannot be undone. The removal of breasts, ovaries and genitals are permanent. But do the President and the politicians really care? Is it just enough to win one more political election or one more candidate for the LGBTQIA+ Community? Do these enabling Presidents, Democrats and Cabinet members care that the lives of minors are ruined just to score a political point with the LGBTQIA+ community for their votes and money?

CHAPTER SIX: DOES GOD HAVE ANY PLACE IN THIS DISCUSSION?

Is it appropriate that God should play a role in the affairs of the nation founded under God? Many years ago, a lot of Americans would have immediately said: "YES"! But today it is very doubtful that many Americans will line up for that "yes" answer. And that is a problem. God has no room in many American homes anymore today for various selfish reasons. America is suddenly and continuously going down in their faith and belief in God. A USA TODAY reporter wrote:

"The percentage of adults in the United States who believe in God has dropped to its lowest point since at least 1944, according to a new survey. Relying on Gallup's long-running survey, Marina Pitofsky of USA TODAY said on June 17, 2022:

"Between the years 1944 and 2011, over 90% of Americans said they believed in God." According to the survey only 42% of Americans said that God can hear people's prayers and intervene on a person's behalf. Ms. Pitofsky went on to say:

"This year, 68% of people ages 18-29 years old said they believe in God. Among people who identified as Democrats, 72% said they believe in God. Among those who identified as liberal, 62% said they believe in God."

When God is driven out of human discourse, people think upside down. Imagine a downgrade from 90% down to 72% or lower today. In another article of June 24, 2022, titled: "How many Americans believe in God?", Lydia Saad and Zach Hrynowski found out:

"Most recently, Gallup found 81% of Americans expressing belief when asked the simple question, "Do you believe in God?" This was down from 87% in 2017 and a record low for this question first asked in 1944, when 96% believed in God. It reached a high of 98% in the 1950s and 1960s." In the same Gallup 79% said they are convinced God exists in 2016 and in 2017 the number goes down to 64%. Gallup measures Americans' views on God and religion as part of its Values and Beliefs Poll – one of 12 surveys that make up the Gallup Poll Social Series."

From the foregoing, the United States is losing faith in God every year. It does not need a soothsayer to find out why. Recently young people have been steadily misinformed and misdirected by politicians, political appointees and some progressive judges, who like to legislate from the bench. The introduction of abortion, transgender and gay lifestyles have been the most destabilizing issues of faith among the growing population of America because they find it difficult to reconcile those unnatural lifestyles and belief in God. Both legalized abortion and gay lifestyle, which are very popular today in America, are all against the laws of God. Many have sold these issues and made them rather attractive issues for young people. When unusual things start happening, the weak and uninformed or not well informed begin to ask if there is really God in the affairs of man. When young people are officially introduced by their government and politicians to the cult of atheism, the culture of death and the gay lifestyle, their belief in the Almighty God begins to erode. When they read or hear about gay bishops like Bishop Gene Robinson, the Episcopal bishop of New Hampshire, some young people lose interest in religion and God. After all these are the adults, the teachers, religious leaders and the leaders of the people, who should know better. When fragile and undeveloped minds in grade schools are officially taught with the permission of the government and adults they respect and look up to, that they can change their sex from boy to girl or girl to boy, they begin to think that the idea of God is no longer relevant as they grow up. Who wants to worship a god that makes one male when the individual should be female? Growing up with that background, some of these young people easily switch off the idea of the God they learnt at home and in the Church. At home and in their Church, they have also been taught to respect life and other people's property as part of the ten Commandments given to humanity by God.

But now they are being introduced to the culture of death through abortion, the culture of "everyone is a god unto himself or herself", through gay lifestyles and transgenderism. Man can make himself anything he wants - man or woman or even no gender at all. Now individuals in the LGBTQAI+ community think they can overrule the Almighty and correct His 'mistakes' by recreating individuals. Young people, especially teens are already at a disadvantaged position as far as sex is concerned. From where they stand, nature seems to work against them in sexual matters unless they have good parents, mentors, friends and other adults around to guide them toward God and Godly things and people. They naturally like to explore and experiment on anything sexual because it is all new to them. That is how young people fall prey to sex predators. Impressionable minds of teens and the young act before they think. But some of these young people, who go ahead and join the squad of the culture of death, perhaps, atheism, gay lifestyle and transgenderism, will eventually discover that it is a losing game. But like spilled milk or gin out of the bottle, they cannot go back into the bottle; it is too late. Likewise, those of them who lineup for irreversible gender mutilation suffer perpetual mind torture and regret after. But at that point, it is too late to put-back together. Since they have lost belief in God, these young people end up thinking of or taking their own lives out of desperation because, at that stage, they have no anchor point in God. As we know, the moral anchor comes from God, whom they have no connection with currently.

The proponents of this madness of alternative lifestyle know this tragedy is one of the possible outcomes of forcing children into 'trans'-euphoria. Yet they continue to introduce the children into it. To save face they try to push and force the so-called "gender affirming care" on parents after the damage has been done as if to say, 'everything will be alright', kid-o. It won't. It hasn't been. The transgender maniacs are aware of the downside of this procedure and still do it anyway to perpetuate the madness. If they don't recruit people into the cult, their kingdom falls. This deliberate invasion of the innocence of young people by some politicians, judges and LGBTQIA+ operatives is the reason why suicide among young trans people in the United States and elsewhere is very high. It is built on a false premise.

According to the National Institute of Mental Health, "suicide is considered the second leading cause of death for adolescents between the ages of 10 and 14, and the third leading cause of death for those between 15 - 24." In 2015, the Center for Disease Control (CDC) also stated that an estimated 9.3 million adults, which is roughly 4% of the United States population, had suicidal thoughts in one year alone. The culture of death and disbelief in God can only bring about more such deaths across the board. It does not stop with the killing of babies in the womb. No! It even affects all the participants, unfortunately. When life is devalued, it becomes easier to shoot to kill others without any prick of conscience because God is no longer in the picture. When human life is officially devalued by the government, politicians and courts, that official act by them, becomes a license for everyday people on the street to act recklessly as if there is no God. Coming from the government, politicians and courts some individuals take it as a license to beat and stab others to death. Subconsciously the ordinary person runs with it that people in power have given them a license to kill. Moreover, there is no accountability for their actions since some of the people in charge do not have a strong belief in God, if at all they do believe. The respect for all human life and people comes from the understanding that life belongs to God and God alone. It is a bit understandable that a few individuals, just a few, will choose to have no respect for God or life. There is no way to understand that the representatives of the people will assume, legislate and adopt a culture of death and disregard for God as a way of life. But if some of our politicians and people who vote for those issues disrespect the lives of babies in the womb, there will be chaos on our streets because life is life in or out of the womb.

Is there any wonder that many aspects of life in America now are going South? To lose grip on God, is to lose grip on reality. Watch the trend on how Americans are losing Faith in God as the years go by since 1973. Watch the trend from the Hippie age and sexual revolution of the sixties and the emergence of homosexuality thereafter and transgenderism of today. Watch how humanity is gradually being debased from rationality and hope to hopelessness and irrational behaviors and resultant depression. Who would have thought a hundred years ago that a man would be married to another man "legally" or that the present generation of teachers would explicitly or otherwise teach their students that there are no standards, no objective values, especially in the Universities. They teach that it is all what you think or want it to be. That by itself puts a big question mark on REASON. The individual's wants supersede God's plan for humanity. That is how belief in God is gradually being washed away in our nation.

For instance, abortion was illegal in the Nation until January 22, 1973, just fifty plus (50+) years ago. Since then, abortion has become more popular as the years go by. According to Pew Research Center, about 61% of American adults say that abortion should be legal in all or most cases, while about 37% say that abortion should be illegal in all or most cases. According to an article published by Hannah Hartig, a research associate focusing on U. S. politics and policy research at Pew Research Center:

"The latest Pew Research Center survey conducted March 7-13, 2022, finds deep disagreement between - and within - the parties over abortion. In fact, the partisan divide on abortion is far wider than it was two decades ago."

She compared the Democrats and Republicans on their leanings on the issue of abortion. In that survey 80% of Democrats and Democratic-leaning independents think that abortion should be legal in all or most cases while 32% think it should be illegal. On the other hand, 72% of Republicans and Republican-leaning independents think that abortion should be illegal in all or most cases while 39% think it should be legal in all or most cases. Between 2007 and 2022 among the Democrats the gap between those who want abortion to be legal and those who don't has grown wider from 33 points to 42 points in favor of abortion while among Republicans the gap has dropped one point against abortion (39% in 2007 to 38% in 2022). As you can see, the disastrous effect is widespread among the two major parties. Thirty nine percent of Republicans support abortion while eighty percent of Democrats support abortion in America. Now abortion decides elections these days. If you are a politician and promise to legalize abortion as an election slogan, you are very likely to win. A lot of Americans who know that abortion takes the life of a baby, still believe that a politician can give them permission to do so. Somehow, they think that politicians making it legal absolves them from guilt even though they know that God said: "Thou shall not kill." It is a mind game that people play. In the same way some politicians, who claim to be religious, say that they personally do not believe in abortion but vote to legalize it for their constituencies. Right! What a shame! Stop the deception, my friend.

Support for legal abortion also varies by race, ethnicity, education and religious affiliation. The comparison among religious groups in the Nation is even more revealing. "White evangelical Protestants continue to be opposed to abortion in all or most cases." Ms. Hartig quoted the survey:

"Nearly three-quarters of White evangelicals (74%) say it should be illegal in all or most cases, while 24% of evangelicals say it should be legal in all or most cases. In contrast, many White Protestants who are not evangelicals (60%) say abortion should be legal in all or most cases. Religious "nones" (- those who are religiously unaffiliated -) overwhelmingly support legal abortion. Over eight in ten (84%) say it should be legal in all or most cases while just 15% say it should be illegal."

In general, 52% of Protestants say abortion should be illegal while 45% say it should be legal. For Catholics 56% say it should be legal while 42% say it should be illegal. Amazing!! That is how bad it has become. Politicians, Judges and religious leaders have a lot to ponder on this issue. The presence of God or lack thereof shapes who the people are, and it shows. This is how America got to where it is today in a state of chaos. People, whom the journalists called the "Nones", are people who say they believe in God but do not have a religious group; that is to say, people who have no anchor to a religious group or family, are more likely to condemn an innocent baby in the womb to death than people who are affiliated to a religious group. Being affiliated to a religious group means that an individual believes in God and has a place and a group of people he or she practices that religion with. With reference to abortion, one not only believes in God, but puts into action that belief in some givens: that God owns life; that God's Commandment forbids us to take away the lives of others etc. Members of a religious group are regularly reminded of God's teachings which are reinforced in practice in religious groups through daily or weekly Church attendance at least. To be a non-affiliate to a group that believes in God means the individual does not want a commitment to God. To claim to believe in God is just enough. It is amazing how lack of faith in God permeates all the other affairs of human behavior. God is the foundation of the structure; without God the structure ruptures and disintegrates into rubles. The absence of God in people's lives brings about societal problems: disintegration of the family; a belief in divorce; teenage crimes, teen pregnancies, teen drug use, teen school dropout, teen gang violence, teen depression, teen suicide; adult alcoholism; adult sexual irresponsibility that fans abortion; gay culture and transgenderism; drag queen culture; perversive mental illness; a culture of death; hopelessness and homelessness. Faithless and stubborn politicians and people spend political lifetimes trying to fix those societal problems, when the answer is simply, belief and close association with God.

CHAPTER SEVEN: GOD, THE FOUNDATION OF THE FAMILY AND COUNTRY

The family is God's first and basic society. It is from the family that human society originates. Without the family there is no society and there is no nation. That is why the family must be morally strong to have a morally strong society and a morally strong nation. If the family is destroyed, society is destroyed as well. The streets become war zones; there is no respect for people's property; crimes abound; life becomes worthless; human beings make themselves better than God by recreating human beings etc. If God is kicked out of the family, there will be no God in society. It is precisely for this reason that all agents of the devil start their societal attack on the family and the young people, who are the future of the family and society. This is why Fatherless homes in America are a dangerous trend. To destroy society, one must destroy the family first through the children of the family, the future of society.

The Founding Fathers of the United States of America understood the place of God in human affairs very well when they formulated the "Declaration of Independence" from Great Britain. The Founding Fathers started the declaration thus:

"We hold these truths to be self-evident, that all men are created equal, that they are endowed by their Creator with certain unalienable Rights, that among these are Life, Liberty and the pursuit of Happiness..." The Founding Fathers of the Nation acknowledged that God is the Creator of everyone. Now some people don't acknowledge that there is God let alone being the Creator. The Founding Fathers concluded with these words:

"We, therefore, the Representatives of the united States of America, in General Congress, Assembled, appealing to the Supreme Judge of the world for the rectitude of our intentions, do, in the Name, and by the Authority of the good people of these Colonies, solemnly publish and declare, That these United Colonies are, and of Right ought to be Free and Independent States; that they are Absolved from all Allegiance to the British Crown, and that all political connection between them and the State of Great Britain, is and ought to be totally dissolved; and that as Free and Independent States, they have full Power to levy War, conclude Peace, contract Alliances, establish Commerce, and to do all other Acts and Things which Independent States may of right do. And for the support of this Declaration, with a firm reliance on the protection of divine Providence, we mutually pledge to each other our lives, our Fortunes and our sacred Honor."

Then all the delegates from the Colonies signed the Declaration for and on behalf of their people. It is evident that the Founding Fathers acknowledged the Supremacy of God, the Creator of all things ("Supreme Judge of the world"). They also relied on "divine Providence" and asked for God's help to achieve their goal to separate from Great Britain. This was on July 4, the year 1776. That was an exhibition of the faith the Founding Fathers of the nation had in themselves and the people of God they represented. America was founded on God, Life, Liberty and pursuit of Happiness. That was then.

But fast forward to 2023 and see a disappointing number of American people who believe in God. It is interesting to note that apart from an explicit mention of God the Almighty, 'Truth' was prominent. "We hold these truths to be self-evident..." Truth, as we know, is the absence of lies or falsehood. That means that truth is real, constant and unchangeable. If one is male, he will always be male and nothing else can change it because it is the truth. That is why transgenderism is a farce and a smoking mirror. Truth got its force and meaning from God, who is the Truth and the Unchangeable. For the same reason, Jesus is the Way, the Truth and the Life. Remember the portion that talks about "Life, Liberty and pursuit of Happiness." Can anyone think of or imagine happiness without God? Without God there is no happiness. That is why America is not at ease today. There is no happiness without God. So, the Founding Fathers made it clear that to succeed, the leaders must recognize the Supremacy of the Creator, that God's Truth which makes us free (Liberty) is the foundation of any nation and finally that those two bring about Happiness. The absence of happiness breeds anger, sadness, dissatisfaction, depression, hatred, hopelessness and evil thoughts of homicide and suicide. The absence of God explains why America is in a different place today. Some of our leaders today have redirected America away from the vision of the Founding Founders of the Nation and the Constitution. American leaders have of late set America on the path of killing our babies in the womb, brought in an alternative lifestyle, which is anti-God by rejecting God's Commandments (one man and one woman to increase and multiply) and usurping God's function of creation by attempting to recreate God's creation in transgenderism and Godlessness, which is the product of the first two. And this is unfortunate.

To understand what is happening in America now, one must understand the place of God in present day America. It is like trying to start a car when there is no fuel in the tank. It is like asking a bunch of four-year-olds to drive a brand-new car with fuel and all. To drive a car successfully, one needs to have a well-functioning car with all that it needs to function and a competent driver, not one or the other but both. There is a need for families and the operating force, which is God, to be the driver who drives the family and the nation. Otherwise, there will be crashes (of crimes, depression, hopelessness and homelessness) all over the place as we are experiencing today in cities and streets of America and all other countries that take their cue from America for direction. The result will be decadence, devaluation and destruction of God's kingdom on earth. Many powerful countries and empires on earth have gone through power, influence and affluence before us. Many countries and empires have been here before. But where are they now? There have been about sixty Empires that are no longer famous today. Let us look at a few of them:

1. The AKKADIAN EMPIRE: (2334 BCE - 2154 BCE)

The Akkadian Empire extended its power, influence and control to all Mesopotamia including modern day Iraq, Syria and Iran. Where is it today? Gone!

1. THE ROMAN EMPIRE: (27 BCE - 476 CE)

The Roman Empire covered vast areas across Europe, and parts of Asia and Africa.

1. THE MONGOLIAN EMPIRE: (1206 CE- 1368 CE)

Controlled territories from Europe to Asia, including parts of China, Russia and Middle East.

1. THE BRITISH EMPIRE: (1583 - 1997)

The British Empire was the most powerful and covered and controlled one quarter of the world's lands.

1. THE UNITED STATES OF AMERICA: (1776 AD -?)

The USA is the leader of the free world, the world's Superpower, with influence all over the world.

And where are these Empires now? They are gone and America is on life support. When they forgot the Creator of the world and thought that their power, influence and affluence would do it, they went by the wayside because "power corrupts, and absolute power corrupts absolutely". America seems to be going that route. When God endows a country with wealth and power and their leaders kick God out of their life and territory, destruction and utter failure follow. Remember that everybody and everything comes from God willing it. To turn around and spit on the face of the source of your power and existence is the height of stupidity.

There was a time in America when Christ was the center of Christmas. Both the old and the young looked forward to Christmas and celebrated it with faith. Now look at what has happened to Christmas in America today where Christ, "the birthday boy", has been kicked out of His birthday celebration by billionaire atheists, who control companies and money. But they love to use His birthday to make money anyway. The original "Merry Christmas" used all over the world for centuries has been replaced with "Happy Holidays". Whose Holiday? Very soon young Americans will not know that there was a time "CHRIST" was in Christmas. With "Happy Holidays", Christmas will be just one of the other holidays of the year in the background. That is one of the most subtle ways of canceling the birth of Christ and Christianity in this age of "cancellation" in America. The meaning of Christmas will soon be lost on the young generation - a slap on Christianity.

We started with kicking God out of the public schools. That, of course, is one of the effects of what happened in the sixties. The chickens of the sixties have come home now in our time to roost. A Godless society is destined to fall. Look at how God pretty much has left America today for the leaders to do whatever they want and face the music later. When the children indoctrinated in the last twenty years begin to run the affairs of government, America will certainly be unrecognizable. It is fast approaching unless some adults in the room step in and save the day.

On June 25,1962 the Supreme Court ruled in Engel v Vitale that government sponsored prayer in public schools is unconstitutional. Let us look at the merits of the Supreme Court's decision. The majority opinion of 6 Justices was written by Hugo L Black in which the majority argued "that, by using its public school system to encourage the recitation of the Regent's prayer, the State of New York has adopted a practice wholly inconsistent with the Establishment Clause." That opinion is not accurate.

Now look at the minority opinion by Justice Potter Stewart, who argued that the majority had "misapplied a great constitution principle" and he could not understand "how an 'official religion' is established by letting those who want to say a prayer say it. On the contrary, I think to deny the wish of these school children to join in reciting this prayer is to deny them the opportunity of sharing in the spiritual heritage of our Nation."

This is sound interpretation and in keeping with the First Amendment. If one looks closely at the two opinions, it will be discovered that Justice Potter Stewart got it right. But before we continue, let us look at the prayer which one could rightly describe as non-denominational; and moreover, the prayer was optional for students to be part of it or not. This was the prayer:

"Almighty God, we acknowledge our dependence upon Thee, and we beg Thy blessings upon us, our parents, our teachers, and our country." Perfect prayer, one would say! Who could object to a prayer which acknowledges God's almighty, asking Him to bless the students, their parents, their teachers and the country? Where is that talking about the establishment of a religion? There was none. Justice Hugo L. Black, in the majority opinion, is the one who infringed on the rights of students to exercise their First Amendment right. The First Amendment of the Constitution states:

"Congress shall make no law respecting an establishment of religion or prohibiting the free exercise thereof;" Justice Hugo Black prohibited the free exercise of students who wanted to pray.

This prayer was to be recited at the beginning of the school day. Does this payer not reflect what the Founding Fathers wrote in the declaration? Where is the establishment of "official religion" in the prayer? That is precisely what Justice Stewart could not see in the prayer, and I don't see it either. Instead, he observed that the majority opinion is denying the students the opportunity to voluntarily exercise their First Amendment right to join or not to join in prayer. That denial is what is unconstitutional. See how the minority opinions in this case and Roe v Wade were spot on in their dissent opinions while the majority opinions in the two cases were on a wild goose chase.

What are the effects of the Engel v Vitale ruling today? That, for sure, produced low morality in schools and society eventually because the schools produced the rulers of today and the society of today. The effect of the absence of prayer in public schools has an incremental lowering of educational standards, an increase of lack of the knowledge of God, no respect for God and authority, an increase in excessive violence and lawlessness in both public schools and society at large. After graduation, students go into society, the real and unsheltered world, to put their education into practice. And this is what we got today. If the six Justices in Engel v Vitale had got it right, there might never have been a Roe v Wade in 1973 or Obergefell v Hodges in 2015.

The Supreme Court could have fashioned their decision in such a way as to stop government or school authorities from abuse of religion and at the same time let government and school authorities offer religious and moral learning and practice in public schools just as we have in some countries of the world, the United States Military, State and Federal prisons. If they had structured public schools like that, students would have been given the opportunity to know God early, learn and practice their own brand of religion just as soldiers, inmates in State and Federal prisons are given the opportunity to learn and practice the religion of their choice. Both the State and Federal governments spend money to hire Chaplains of different religions to teach and conduct religious services for the inmates and soldiers as a right under the First Amendment (prohibiting the exercise thereof). In the military and prisons in this country no one is forced to study or practice any religion. But the opportunity is given to soldiers and inmates to learn about God and worship Him the way the inmates or soldiers know how at the direction of the Chaplains of their faith. That is what one would have expected from the Supreme Court in Engel v Vitale. Students would have had the opportunity to know and love God to the best of their knowledge and exposure at an early age to function in society as God fearing and law-abiding citizens of society. These young students would have learned about good and bad and the consequences of doing either in the same environment where they learn mathematical equations and grammatical principles and laws of physics. Students would see the knowledge and practice of religion as important as the other subjects like English, Science and Mathematics. It is only when every student is given the opportunity to know and love God, that the society will feel and experience the presence of God in the youngest members of society. Irrespective of their religious affiliation, students who were raised in the love and fear of God would not engage in doing hard drugs to numb their brains to commit crimes or wearing baggy clothes where they hide guns, which they use to kill teachers and fellow students. Contrast that with private and religious schools where the students learn about God and religion. In those schools, there are dress codes and discipline appropriate to young people. More importantly we would have had morally balanced people in politics today if all of them were trained in schools where God was present.

There are other countries which adopt a slightly different method of introducing God to the students at an early stage at the place where students learn to read and write. In the same environment where they learn English, Mathematics and the Sciences, they also learn about God. This is how some countries do it. The Ministry of Education mandates Principals to inform and invite all the religious leaders in the area where the school is situated for a meeting. A day and time every week are chosen when all the religious or denominational leaders could come into the school grounds, take their religious adherents to a classroom or designated place and teach them the morality and practice of their religion or denomination. Even then students are free to attend or not. In doing so the students realize the importance of God as well as education in their lives 12 years before they go to college. These governments do this because they realize that morally trained students and God-fearing students produce good citizens later.

When we remove God out of the discussion in human affairs, there is bound to be chaos. What follows is that the individual puts himself or herself or sex or drugs or power in the place of God. When such people become superior to God, they begin to assume Godly functions like recreating human beings and reapportioning genders to themselves or others. That is what is now trending in our public schools. Ignorant and unassuming ten, eleven-year-olds in our public schools are groomed, educated and morally coerced to change their universally accepted pronouns by some school authorities, who are paid with the taxpayers' money. With the help of public-school workers, students go through body mutilations in the name of transgenderism without any permission from parents. How does anyone think this story will have a good ending especially when the Biden government is fanning the flames of anti-religion and anti-God behaviors? What a stupid move! Unfortunately for the United States of America, that is where we are heading to if that government does not change course vis a vis God and morality in this country. It is not too late to change course, revisit Engel v Vitale case, reinstate family and God in their positions to let respect, peace and harmony reign in America again. If this happens, all the countries that emulate the United States of America, will follow suit and the world would become a better place. Without the foundation, there is no solid building; God is the foundation; without God, there is no solid family, no solid Nation.

CHAPTER EIGHT: POLYGAMY, BIGAMY & POLYANDRY ACCOMMODATION

POLYGAMY:

What is polygamy? Polygamy is defined as the practice of having more than one spouse at the same time and everybody involved knows everybody in the arrangement. It is mostly used in Africa where this exercise was common, to describe a situation when a man has more than one wife at the same time. The women involved usually know each other and most of the time willingly agree to marry one man and co-exist as co-wives in the marriage. In a lot of cases, it starts with one woman. After several years, the man may introduce a second wife to the family. In some cases, with the principal wife the man goes to do the required rites to bring the second wife home. After a few years again a third and maybe fourth wife comes into the family. The wives sometimes agree to live together, and the children are trained by all the wives. In some situations, the wives have a division of labor in doing things for the whole family in the house and the first wife oversees this. The family works together, plays and eats together. In other situations, each wife does her own thing having a responsibility only to the husband and her children.

In some situations, the idea of marrying a second or third wife is not planned. Sometimes it starts when the man sees himself in some circumstance where he sees polygamy as a solution to a problem. The couple may not have any children, or they do not have a male child, who will take the place of his father when he joins his ancestors. This is a serious situation in Africa where a family without a son is not respected. Sometimes in that scenario, it is the first wife that introduces the idea of a second wife to her husband to get another wife to rescue the family. It may even be the first wife who introduces a second wife to her husband. One such example is in the Old Testament when Sarah gave her Egyptian maid to her husband, Abram, as a second wife because she had no child.

In any case all the women agree to live together with one husband even though things don't work out well in some cases, just as things don't always work out in some one man one wife marriages. Of course, there are some polygamous families where the man unilaterally brings in a second or third wife home and forces everybody to live together. Whatever the situation, polygamy has to do with one man marrying many wives. While this form of marriage was acceptable in Africa and some other parts of the world, it is illegal in the United States of America.

POLYANDRY:

There is another form of marriage which is not one man marrying one woman. It is called polyandry. This is when a woman has more than one husband at the same time and all the men in the relationship are aware that they are sharing the love of one woman. This arrangement is very rare, but it exists. Like polygamy, polyandry starts with the central figure, which in this case is the woman. It could start by the woman soliciting the love of the men. Like the man, in a polygamous marriage, the woman can start with one man and progress to two or three or more. Everything is worked out as a group and the children are taken care of as a group. In this relationship the woman is the controller and head of the family. Like polygamy, polyandry is accepted in some parts of the world. But it is not an African thing. It is also illegal in the United States of America.

BIGAMY:

Bigamy is when a man or a woman has more than one spouse and the other spouse has no knowledge of another or the others in the relationship. In that kind of a relationship one partner is hiding facts about the marriage from the other partner. It starts with an official and recognized marriage between a man and a woman and somewhere along the line, one partner, invariably the man, establishes another permanent sexual relationship, sometimes with children, unknown to his wife. Sometimes, the man for instance, would want a male child from the hidden lady/spouse when the first wife does not have a son. However, that whole arrangement would be regarded as deception on the part of the man. Bigamy is not a marriage relationship in the real sense because it involves a deception which makes the relationship illegal in many countries including the United States of America. It could be likened to an extended extra-marital affair or adultery. Is the United States of America considering elevating bigamy to the altar of 'protected class'? If not, why not?

Now where is the United States of America about polygamy, polyandry and bigamy? Is America ready to legalize these relationships now that the marriage goal post has been moved to accommodate gay marriage? The acceptance of gay marriage was because of some coordination of their members in high political positions, the judiciary, and others in the corridors of power and several demonstrations over the years. With a lot of money, they bought their way to where they are now, at the center table contributing to decision making in government. What if there is another rebellion like the "Stonewall rebellion" by one or all these marriage categories above seeking recognition as a minority group? Then what, Supreme court, Congress and of course, America? Then what?

All over the world there are thousands of women in polygamous marriages who say they are happy in their marriages with two, three, four up to ten co-wives or sister wives with many children in the big family. What is wrong with American women getting the opportunity of experimenting on polygamy, bigamy or polyandry? Yes, a group in the State of Utah tried it. They said they were happy and seemed to be happy with it. We are talking about the men of the members of the Church of Jesus Christ of Latter-day Saints who married more than one wife. None of the women involved was complaining. What did the United States of America do to them? The government has laws against polygamy in the country, and they enforced the law. Many men went to prison for marrying more than one wife. In the Old Testament men married many wives and it was legal. From all indications the individuals involved seemed to be as happy as in today's one man one wife marriages.

Even today there are thousands of men who say they are happy to coexist in a marriage relationship with several other men and one woman. What the Federal government is doing with recognizing gay marriages has a lot of ramifications that it cannot squarely face or accommodate. What if all or some of the Muslim men in the United States of America, and they are in the millions, were to demonstrate or rebel in favor of marrying multiple women according to the Muslim religion, would America deny them that "civil right" of marrying the multiple women they say they "love", just as the gays and lesbians have been accommodated because they say they "love" their partners? How could anybody dare deny their request when they say that they are "in love"? Granted there is a law against polygamy, for instance; so also, there was a law against homosexuality (Sodomy laws) in the United States. Now all laws against homosexuality are history. Is America ready to recognize all the other groups just as the homosexual group is recognized? That is the question. One of the reasons the gay group uses the term "love" is that two people who are in "love" (man and man or woman and woman) should be allowed to marry. The same argument could go for a Muslim man who "loves" two or more up to four women, according to their Koran. Since what is good for the goose is good for the gander, groups in a polygamous, polyandrous and bigamous relationships should be recognized as legitimate forms of marriage in these United States of America. If a man could validly marry another man because of the said "love", why can a Muslim in the United States not marry many wives in accordance with the Islamic law citing the same "love"? This should apply to any man who wants to marry multiple women who agree to be in such a relationship.

It is amazing how intelligent men and women become irrational sometimes to defend a political agenda or ideology. If the United States of America can find a reason to officially recognize same sex marriage, as unnatural as it is, how can it oppose polygamy in the State of Utah and elsewhere in the United States? Many of the men in polygamous relationships in the State of Utah were or are still in prison for relationships, which, though unchristian, are not unnatural like gay marriages. It boggles the mind to even think of the irrationality of the American government and Justices defending and promoting the LGBTQIA+ community at the expense of even Christian values on which the nation was founded. It was not enough that a gay culture has been officially introduced and adopted in America; the wheels of government of late are manipulated by the gay community. Almost all the departments and agencies of the Federal government are run or deputized, at some level, by the gay community, which is more anti-religion than polygamy could be. Polygamy believes in and promotes life and children while gay lifestyle is anti-children and procreation. Polygamy is for 'increase and multiply' of the Bible while the gay culture is anti-procreation in a practical and real sense.

Same sex marriage has been recognized as a sexual preference for some Americans as a civil right under the First Amendment and the Fourteenth Amendment. That is weird, though. Is the Supreme Court ready to recognize the marriage of some Americans, whose sexual preference or orientation is having multiple wives or multiple husbands? Is the Supreme Court ready to accept bestiality as an acceptable marriage relationship and a civil right also? What would be their reason for not granting a person permission to get married to his or her dog as the "love" of his or her life? Where do the courts and congress draw the line? Once the gin is out of the bottle, it is hard to put it back. The Supreme Court spilled the gin, can it put it back in the bottle?

PROTECTED GROUPS AND HYPOCRISY:

In 1973, the Supreme Court of the United States of America granted women the permission to get rid of the babies in their womb if they so desire. How about so many other Americans who have other, perhaps objectionable desires that are not abortion? The one deliberate blunder of legitimizing abortion, in my opinion, dislocated the moral equilibrium of the United States of America up till this day. Despite the moral decadence America has experienced since Roe v Wade and the flagrant disregard for life among the young people on our streets, the Democrats and the Biden administration are still using abortion as their election gift and number one slogan for the 2024 campaign. They prefer doubling down on the culture of death in the womb and on the streets of America to win an election than saving lives in the womb and streets of America. What happens to prosperity, safe streets, the American dream, peace at home and abroad and strong family and family values? Why are they not campaigning on those issues as their achievement in government? They cannot because there is no prosperity, no safe streets, no American dream, no peace at home and abroad, no strong family and no family values.

If the courts were to deny these marriage sub-groups if those groups were to seek protective class status, it would be the height of injustice. But if on the other hand they recognize bestiality, bigamy, polygamy and polyandry as legitimate forms of marriages and alternate lifestyles, what would this country look like in the end? A free for all country where so called "Freedom" reigns? The Founding Fathers of the United States of America who were intelligent, good and decent people, would be rolling in their graves because of the way we have abused "Freedom". When they introduced the word Freedom they didn't mean freedom from common sense; they didn't mean freedom from responsibility and decency. They didn't mean that freedom was anarchy and lawlessness. They used freedom in context; freedom to do the right and decent thing. Here is a little history to clarify the misunderstanding some people have about freedom.

The Founding Fathers of the United States looked at the status quo in Europe where they fled from. In Europe at the time, the king or queen had the power to force people to do whatever he or she commanded just because they said so. People were forced to believe in the one religion the king or queen practiced without any accommodation for other people with other religions. There was no freedom of religious practice because the king or queen had the last word on what religion the subjects practiced. Persecution or death was the penalty for the subject's non-compliance. They called it, "The Divine Right of Kings" as if it came from God. So, in Europe at the time what was being practiced was described with this Latin phrase: "Cuius regio, eius religio", which literally means: "whose realm or territory, their religion". In other words, it means that he who governs the territory decides the territory's religion or that the job of the ruler was to dictate or determine the religion of the people he rules. It was this practice and tradition that drove some Europeans, who had different religious views, to come to America to escape persecution from Monarchs in Europe. This practice in Europe then laid the foundation for the freedoms proposed by the Founding Fathers in the United Colonies/States of America. That was the foundation of the Bill of Rights, the first of which were the Rights of the First Amendment, of which the Freedom of Religion was one of them. Both the legalization of abortion and gay marriage were linked to the First Amendment and equal protection by the Justices.

In their new country, they were still British subjects. But when the oppression that made them leave Great Britain (or Europe) took the form of taxation without representation, the Colonies declared their independence to become the United States of America in 1776. That was why Freedom took center stage in the Amendments and was the main point in the First Amendment of the Constitution. The freedoms of the First Amendment had context and were limited by common sense and reason. It was not meant to be freedom to kill your neighbor or steal his goods because you don't like his face. It did not mean freedom to shout "Fire" in a crowded theater just because one has the freedom of the first Amendment to shout. The Freedom we have in the First Amendment does not mean freedom to ditch our God given faculty of reason, to believe what does not make sense. The Founding Fathers wanted us to use our God- given faculty of reasoning and apply it to the freedoms of the First Amendment. That means that we do not exercise the freedom to shout "fire" in a crowded theater because reason is supposed to tell us the mayhem, stampede and death that would cause, for instance. At the same time, it does not make sense for any American to kill his neighbor because he does not like his face. There are hundreds or even thousands of people who don't like the faces of other thousands of people and that may include you. If all these people are allowed to kill them off because they have the freedom of the First Amendment, how many people will be left in America? This is why "reason" must be part of the decisions of the First Amendment. That explains why God gave us reasoning at a certain age in life. Do our lawyers, Judges, and politicians think about the role of reason in the exercise of their duties to administer justice to the American people? When an attorney claims First Amendment Right in court the judge should weigh the claim against reason.

Here are some examples from American transgender world that questions reasoning and common sense:

1. A transgender adult on the anniversary of his sex "change" said:

   "I am celebrating my first birthday".

1. A similar case is when a woman, who is either a member of the gay community or sympathetic to their cause said:

   "My transgender son is pregnant".

Let us look at those two statements and weigh them against reason and truth. Let us see if any of those statements pass the test of reason.

Knowledge, as we know, is an agreement between the intellect (inside us/ the knower) and the object (outside the intellect/what is known). Truth is determined when what is posited outside (the statement or the object) corresponds with what the intellect knows (inside). There must be an agreement between the intellect which the speaker has and the object the speaker presents outside (the statement). If there is no agreement, either the object the speaker presents is faulty or the speaker did not see or read the object accurately or he is purposely misrepresenting the object. In either case, there is falsehood and should not be trusted.

Now let us try to analyze the two statements above concerning "transgenderism" which has been approved by Democrats and the Biden and Obama governments.

1st Scenario: In the first scenario a grown-up person (within the age of reason) claims that the first anniversary of his trans gendering is his "first birthday".

When a grown-up man claims that his first birthday is one year of his becoming a "woman", he disowns all those years when he "was" a man before his surgery. It appears he disowns all the years he lived as a man. That is denying reality; that is denying the truth because his intellect tells him and tells us as well that he was twenty or thirty years before he decided to have this surgery. There is no agreement between what the intellect knows about him and his age and the claim "she" made about her so-called "first birthday". Her claim of a first birthday is as false as his claim that he is now a woman because his intellect tells him that he is still a man irrespective of what parts of his body are mutilated because there is no agreement between what the intellect knows (and she also knows) and what she claims in her statement regarding his first birthday.

2nd Scenario: In the second scenario the woman claims that her son is pregnant. Let us analyze that. That statement is incongruous. The intellect (inside her) knows something differently from what is claimed (outside the intellect). She, as an adult, knows that the person she purposely chose to call "son" is a daughter who can get pregnant. On the other hand, she also knows that a man does not get pregnant (through her intellect and what she sees outside in her daughter). Yet she, for some reason, claims that her son is pregnant (outside). Therefore, there is no truth to her claim because there is no agreement between what her intellect tells her and what she presents to people outside. This claim by an adult that her son is pregnant, can only be described as a "childish fantasy and make-belief", which is as true as "the tooth fairy" or Christmas "Santa Claus", "The Chinny" and Santa Claus "North Pole" trip. If it wasn't stupid, it could have been funny.

The two adults in these cases purposely deny the truth and the worst part is that they know they are lying not only to the people but to themselves as well. The last part is the worst because it is intellectual dishonesty to lie to oneself. The two cases do not make sense placed side by side with "reason".

But today in America, the LGBTQ+ people want us to agree that they make 'sense' under the new and "refurbished freedom" of the First Amendment, which the Biden administration and courts also believe. For some agendas, it is the same Court that ignored the reality of the existence of a child in the womb that has also denied the reality that male and female are the only two genders God created. It is the same courts and governments that would not rightly, accommodate and celebrate "polygamy, polyandry or bigamy" months of visibility, but would, of course, wrongly accommodate and celebrate "pride month" for LGBTQIA+ people, for instance. Let us challenge this government to declare one month as "polygamy month" or "polyandry month" or "bigamy month" in America to demonstrate and celebrate Freedom as well as diversity, equity and inclusion (DEI), which the LGBTQIA+ community is propagating too. Where is "diversity, equity and inclusion" (DEI) for Polygamy, Polyandry and Bigamy in America where these are not accommodated? Nowadays everybody uses freedom, civil rights and DEI to suit their own selfish make-beliefs and experimentation. Just to be in power and for political expediency some of our politicians embrace these anomalies but vehemently fight other nations who do far less egregious things like the so-called "child labor" policy or "cruelty to animals" as practiced in other nations. While child labor is not ideal, it is not as unnatural as gay marriage. This is pure hypocrisy. America even challenges the "One child" policy in China with a straight face. What is the difference between the United States' "abortion" and China's "one child" policy? With what is happening in America now, how can one defend those hypocritical positions under the framework of our freedom?

Talking about Freedom, what about the freedom to dissent from accepting gay marriages and legal abortion? Are people free to do that without being called names, maligned and persecuted by the Democrats and Biden administration's DOJ and FBI? Shouldn't freedom work both ways? Can one have the same freedom to disagree with the government and the courts about "abortion" and "gay marriage"? Is that too much to ask for? If the proponents of this new freedom really believe in it, why would it be wrong for a black American to exercise that same freedom to choose to vote for a Democrat or not? Do you remember the famous Biden exchange with a black American who said he would not vote for him again:

"If you are not sure whether to vote for me or Trump, you aren't black", said President Biden.

The question now is: Is it the truth and reality that matter or what works just for me, the individual in power? In their hypocrisy the Biden government and some politicians, because of their "climate agenda", want to stop other nations from eating as much beef as they want because of "climate change enthusiasts" on the left of the Democratic party who claim that cows pollute the climate while they themselves cannot do without their 'bacon' for breakfast, 'hamburger' for lunch, 'New York steak' for dinner. The same hypocritical politicians talk about depriving ordinary Americans of the little amenities left in their homes in the name of "climate change" and the "new green deal". To make themselves happy, these political New Green Deals fanatics, want the ordinary Americans, who are not sure of the next meal, to change their old stove, refrigerators etc for new green deal compliant equipment. On top of that they want 'barely making it' Americans, to abandon their fossil fuel cars and buy new, expensive, electric cars, which are not functional, at least, to ordinary Americans, who have only one car to their name, while they, "the political elite" drive multiple cars with multiple bodyguards in multiple cars. During winter months, the political elites can change cars when the electric cars are not functional. Many of the same guardians of the climate, travel in their private planes, which pollute the air several times over. The same government has influenced the United Nations, which is run by liberals, to adopt the "New Green Deal" for the whole world, rich and poor. Hypocrisy!!!

Recently the United Nations condemned the production of livestock in the world while they ate beef for dinner that same day after their meeting. This is hypocrisy in overdrive. If the American people cannot exercise the Freedom to eat or not eat beef, where is the freedom? How would our politicians and power players here deal with any world dictator who uses the same "Freedom" to justify the way they maltreat their people? Those in power in Iran, Russia, North Korea and of course, China, think they have the "freedom" to govern any way they want. It is like the "Divine Right of Kings" scenario in Europe hundreds of years ago. For them it is their "God given freedom" to treat their subjects as slaves. Their actions, we can somehow understand because they are dictators; but what we cannot understand is how our democratic government, where nobody tells others what and when to buy something, is becoming dictatorships where there is no rule of law. That is confusing to a lot of Americans when they see their leaders using the word freedom just as the dictators would use it.

If the powers that be in the United States of America have allowed a "man" in this country to subjectively claim that he could now transition to be a "woman" through surgery or just because he said so and if permission could be given by the same government that it is lawful for a man to marry and have sex with another man in the name of Freedom, what else could be denied to practically anybody in the United States of America? If the government and the courts are allowed to do all that under the umbrella of freedom, why not allow and recognize people who would want to marry their siblings, (remove incest in American dictionary), marry their animal pets, or marry as many wives and husbands as they want? Isn't what is good for the goose, good for the gander anymore? This is how one deliberate blunder made years ago in Roe v Wade, begets other blunders of present-day America. But where do we draw the line as a civilized people, is the question? There are men who sexually "love" other men; there are women who sexually "love" other women; there are men and women who sexually "love" underage children (pedophilia); there are men and women who sexually "love" different kinds of animals and pets; there are American men who like to rape women; there men and women who like to steal and loot property. What should we do with them? Legalize their inordinate tendencies? To continue the blunders shouldn't this government and the courts recognize them all as forms of relationships under the equal protection clause of the First Amendment? If not, why not? You can see that the courts and some politicians have opened the door to something bizarre and we are now stuck with it. How do we get out of the mess? The only thing to do is to go back to our God given reasoning faculty and start thinking and reasoning again. We know we had it before the powers that be introduced "nonsense" and shot down commonsense and reasoning in our political system.

CHAPTER NINE: THE OFFICIAL BIRTH OF ABORTION IN AMERICA

January 22, 1973, is a day of infamy in the United States of America. It is a day that abortion officially became legal in the fifty states of America. Many states had it on their books that willful abortion was illegal. That status quo was tested in Dallas County, Texas by Ms. Norma McCorvey, a 25-year-old woman pregnant with her third child. When the case to abort her baby was denied by the Texas court, she appealed to the Supreme Court of the United States of America. In the suit Norma was given a pseudonym Jane Roe to hide her identity and the Dallas District attorney who defended the case was Henry Wade - hence Roe versus Wade.

On January 22, 1973, the Supreme Court of the United States of America, not the American people through a referendum, not through an Act of Congress, ruled in favor of Norma McCorvey making abortion legal in the whole nation. That conclusion was reached by 7 overzealous Justices out of 9 Justices of the Supreme Court in Roe versus Wade. Why do we say overzealous? The seven Justices knew or should have known that they had no "locus standi" (jurisdiction) in the case. It did not belong to the Supreme court at all; yet they chose to drag themselves where they did not belong for their own personal reasons. Ordinarily Justices interpret the Constitution and laws passed by Congress and signed by the president. Congress did not pass any law about abortion and there was no mention of abortion in the Constitution. Since the American Constitution did not say anything about abortion and Congress did not pass any law regarding abortion, what were the seven Justices interpreting? How can the 7 Justices interpret what is not in the Constitution and not in any law passed by Congress? If they were humble enough, they would have asked the plaintiff to take her case to politicians, who could perhaps raise it in the House and Senate. Perhaps the two bodies could have made some law about it. In that case it would have involved the whole of America through their representatives instead of seven men in the Supreme court. Both the House and Senate would have had vigorous debates on the matter, realizing that they were there because the people put them there and could remove them too if they didn't do justice in the case. The Roe v Wade decision has enabled politicians, Planned Parenthood and lawyers into doing things that have negatively affected the lives of many Americans and of course, the lives of millions of innocent babies killed in legalized abortion in America since 1973.

On that fateful day of January 22, 1973, Justice Harry A. Blackmun, who wrote the majority opinion, told Americans that restricting abortion was unconstitutional. They dragged privacy and the Fourteenth Amendment into it as the reason to make abortion legal. One would think that the Fourteenth Amendment dealt with forceful searches and seizures of a citizen's property without due process. The majority opinion made their conclusion based on the First Amendment and the Fourteenth Amendments. But in his minority opinion, Justice Rehnquist, wrote:

"Even if there were a plaintiff in this case capable of litigating the issue which the Court decides, I would reach a conclusion opposite to that reached by the Court. I have difficulty in concluding, as the Court does, that the right of "privacy" is involved in this case."

And it is not. Justice Rehnquist believes that the plaintiff had no case in the Supreme Court vis a vis Roe V Wade. The Justices would have refused to hear the case. Justice Rehnquist did not believe that Ms. Norma could litigate the case. Many years after Renquist's death, the Supreme Court reversed Roe v Wade on that fact and sent it back to the States where it was before Ms. Norma went to the Supreme Court. It was not a Constitutional matter and had nothing to do with privacy or the Fourteenth Amendment.

However, in the majority opinion in Roe v Wade, Justice Blackmun and the other six Justices, knowing that the majority opinion was flawed, started to look for an avenue of escape by handing to the States the freedom to limit the time abortion could lawfully take place in their respective states. What? Now the majority realized that the case they grabbed and decided belonged to the states. Why did the majority give this responsibility to the states? They also realized that the privacy argument was faulty. They had to find another way to make their argument stick. They also introduced the "fetus" and "personhood" argument by making a distinction between "fetus" and "person". In other words, they started to split hair to the point that they had to ask the States to determine when a fetus becomes a human being or a person.

That, philosophically, will make us ask: what is "being"? Being can be defined as the quality or state of having existence. It refers to the state of being or existing. Does a baby in the womb have existence? Is a baby in the womb a living organism or not? No reasonable person, scientist or not, would say a baby in the womb, at any stage, is not a living organism, an existing and living being separate from the mother. If what the abortion doctor extracts from the womb is not an existing, living organism enjoying being and existence, why not leave it there and see what it becomes; what it is then, human, plant, stone or nothing? This is the job the Supreme Court gave to the States to determine to save face. They did not want to do it themselves because their decision did not make sense.

The question is: Unless there was a conspiracy to interfere with the natural process of development through killing or abortion, what else could a fetus in the womb become? Of course, if attacked, the "fetus" will die just as any of us would die, if people conspire to kill us. But that Court recognized us as persons. Even so-called persons do die when people conspire to kill them. The so-called fetus, like any organism, becomes and develops. Even as a baby outside the womb, the process of becoming continues to adulthood. A newborn baby (person) does not do a lot of things adult persons do. A few months' old baby, though recognized by the seven Justices as a person, does not jump, run or take care of himself as adult persons do. So why did that Supreme Court make the fifty states, fifty gods to determine when a fetus becomes a person? More importantly, why did the Seven Justices not make that determination themselves and tell Americans when life begins since they seem to suggest that life does not begin at conception? If their argument makes sense to abortionists and their supporters, could they tell us whom God told the exact moment life begins other than conception? How can the states make the determination and tell us the moment of the transition from "nothing" to "personhood"; is it 2 or 3 or 4 or 9 months? Even abortionists abort at 9 months. But in their majority opinion, the damage had been done when they decided that abortion was legal. By that pronouncement the seven Justices removed "Thou shalt not kill" from God's Ten Commandments. The American people were empowered to kill innocent and helpless children without qualms. Killing of innocent people in the womb and by extension, on the streets became legal and official in America to a point that politicians use it now as a campaign slogan every election cycle. Such politicians would promise the electorate to keep abortion on the books and decriminalize the killing of babies in the womb if the electorate would vote for them. That permission to kill babies in the womb emboldened street gangs and home burglars that they can as well kill anybody they choose to kill because those people are "unwanted" as far as they were concerned. Street gangs, the mafia and all other killers, reason that if life was sacred, the government would not continue to give permission and funding for the killing of innocent babies.

The Supreme Court of the United States had given victory to Norma McCorvey. But ironically, she later saw what the seven Justices could not see. Like Justices Rehnquist and Scalia, Norma McCorvey (Jane Roe) concluded that what she asked the Court to do in 1973 was not lawful because she realized that the baby she wanted to abort at that stage, had the same value as her two other children. She became a formidable force in the Pro-Life movement later in life. After all she did give birth to that baby. She loved that baby like the rest of her children. That child, after all, was a human being and a person after all.

There is a group of Americans who want permission to kill their babies in the womb without prosecution by the Government as well as those who support them. They are aware that abortion is against the law of God, nature and the State. Why did these women not secretly do it as an adulterer or a murderer or thieves would commit murder, adultery and theft and other sins secretly. In each case people did what they did knowing that it was a prohibited act especially because they have reached the age of reason. This has been a prohibited act for over a century in the United States of America as a nation. This was the understanding in the United States of America for many years before Roe v Wade on January 22nd of 1973, when 7 unelected Justices of the Supreme Court made abortion legal. From that infamous day, abortion became legal and official in America; from that day killing innocent children became official; from that day men and women were given the license to become promiscuous, knowing that if pregnancy occurred, it was legal to kill the baby. The protection of babies in the womb has always been respected everywhere in the world even though some people sometimes have infringed on the law as human beings have always done secretly with all the other commandments of the law for centuries. That is the human condition and human weakness. In the case of America, the law protecting the baby in the womb was part of the American jurisprudence for over a hundred years of its existence. That protection was removed by Roe v Wade in 1973. Acknowledgement of sin and the shame for sin is the reason human beings hide when they offend God by committing sin. But now human beings are challenging and confronting God by declaring legal what He declares illegal.

Pro Abortion Groups:

Under the umbrella of the First Amendment, we have a group of Americans who want the killing of innocent babies in the womb to enjoy the protection of the law as a protected group.

Those Americans are championed by a group called: "Planned Parenthood." The history of the Planned Parenthood of America tells a lot more stories than the group would make people believe. Its name is also deceptive to a lot of unsophisticated American women, who are told that the group is for women's health. But in fact, about 90 percent of the work of Planned Parenthood is abortion. Abortion is the main reason for its existence. But they won't tell us that because "Planned Parenthood" is a very fancy name that sounds family friendly and family oriented. The members enjoy the privilege of existence while they condemn children in the womb to death and declare them "unwanted" or unfit to exist. Planned Parenthood of America tells people that it exists to offer health services to women. So, how is killing a healthy child in the womb a "health care service" to women? Nine times out of ten, this group is involved with abortion on women who come to their clinic. Planned Parenthood of America showed its color during the Democratic National Convention in Chicago, 2024. As its contribution to elect Kamala Harris, the Planned Parenthood of America set up a mobile clinic a few blocks from the Democratic National Convention (DNC) Center in Chicago for free abortion and free vasectomy. This group gathers doctors and nurses, whom they pay very well to dispose of the so-called "unwanted children" in the womb. To make their services look more genuine and attractive, they do not charge most of the women for abortion, especially minority women. Some of the politicians make money available to Planned Parenthood to offer women free and legal abortions any time and on demand. That is how Planned Parenthood of America gets all the money it needs to continue its deadly mission camouflaged as "women's healthcare services". Apart from foundations like George Soros' "Open Society Foundation", Rockefeller's Foundation, Bill and Melinda Gates, Mike Bloomberg, Sheryl Sandberg and other Foundations, Planned Parenthood of America also canvasses and lobbies Congress for money for the so-called "women's Healthcare Services". Before the government and courts got involved with the issues of abortion, Planned Parenthood had gone far into it. But wait to see why the founder was interested in killing babies in the womb.

The Planned Parenthood organization was started by Margaret Sanger in 1939. (Does that date ring a bell?) She was an Obstetric nurse with three children of her own. She was particularly interested in contraceptives for women to prevent births and she coined the name "birth control" in 1914. After her arrest for opening the nation's first birth control clinic in 1916, she founded the "American Birth Control League" the predecessor to Planned Parenthood four years later. (She must know people in the corridors of power.) She was closely connected with a popular group that wanted to "improve" human population by controlling reproduction of human beings. That sounds like what Hitler and his group were doing in Germany to maintain the so-called "pure race" which was also linked with "White Supremacy" and "Racism". From her writings, letters and utterances Margaret Sanger was a racist, who wanted to stop African American children from being born into the world. Most of her clinics were in the poor black neighborhoods of African Americans to control black populations. Ms. Sanger did not want black children because they were not a "pure" race. She loved and praised Germany for their policy of "Eugenics" in 1934. In praise of Germany's sterilization programming in 1934, Margaret Sanger wrote:

"I admire the courage of a government that takes a stand on sterilization of the unfit ..." We now know that Ms. Sanger was not after the health care of women, as her followers claim. She wanted only the "blue blood" to exist.

Margaret Sanger was honored by her supporters with her name being prominently displayed especially on her New York Manhattan Planned Parenthood Clinic, which was established on December 15, 1916. (She died in 1966.) But recently it was announced that her name would be removed by her supporters, July 21, 2020. TIME carried the news:

"On Tuesday, Planned Parenthood of Greater New York announced that it would be removing the name of Margaret Sanger, the organization's founder, from the group's Manhattan clinic. The Name removal is part of the organization's "public commitment to reckon with its founder's harmful connection to the eugenics movement," according to a press release. Planned Parenthood will also work with the City Council and community members to strip nearby Margaret Sanger Square of that name - a designation they (the City Council) had initially pushed for. Time went on:

"Planned Parenthood, like many other organizations that have existed for a century or more, is reckoning with our history, and working to address historical inequities to better serve patients and our mission," Melanie Roussell Newman, senior Vice President of Communications and Culture for Planned Parenthood Federation of America, said in a statement. Ms. Newman also said that the national organization supports the New York Chapter's decision to remove the name. This is the founder of the infamous Planned Parenthood Federation of America.

Margaret Sanger and her foundation deceived most Americans about her real intentions. She was a white supremist and racist. Yes, the current Planned Parenthood has decided to remove her name from their building, but the organization is still operating what they described as the "Founder's harmful connection to the eugenics movement" by all intents and purposes. They are still aborting minority babies in nine out of ten patients. The only reason they made this move to remove their mentor's name from the building was because they were forced by the "Black Lives Matter" (BLM) movement in 2020. So, their action really has no meaning because they are still killing black babies in black neighborhoods free of charge, Margaret Sanger's name on the building or not. Democrat politicians are still making use of her infamous legacy every election year to win elections. The culture of death is still their goal even though the name of the group hides their mission.

This latest move to remove Margaret Sanger's name from the Manhattan building has not stopped politicians and the Foundation from using the clinics as their talking points to win women voters and performing abortions on demand. The official introduction and endorsement of abortion in America by politicians is alive and well. African American politicians and black women till this day, think that organizations like Planned Parenthood are doing them a favor by helping them abort their babies for free. Between them and the abortion doctors a lot of money is realized and spent especially on Black women to curtail the number of children in the black neighborhoods. Over the years this enterprise has become a marriage between the ideology (Margaret's lifelong desire and work) and greed for money (on the part of abortion doctors and nurses). Remove the money incentive, the ideology which started it will drastically flop. Many of the women who patronize the clinics will stop if abortion is no longer free; promiscuity and teenage illicit sex will be minimized; the doctors and nurses will equally look for more paying jobs elsewhere if their pay is cut for lack of funds. It is the billionaires and politicians who are fanning the flames of abortion today. When those college students and women who cannot pay for abortion regularly find out that it is no longer free to have abortions because of lack of funds, they will quickly be forced to decide to stop being sexually reckless. That will save some babies. Abortion at the rate it has climbed in America now is all about money for doctors, election and reelection for politicians. If the funds were to run dry, it would at least cut down on abortion and its collateral, which is youth violence and lives lost on our streets through devaluation of life and the youths desensitized by abortion.

WHY WOMEN WANT ABORTION:

Every human being who has attained the age of reasoning can distinguish between right and wrong. It is natural and innate. Then why do we still do bad things which we know are wrong? It can be traced back to the Fall of human nature and the weakening of our reasoning faculty.

To commit a wrong action which our intellect tells us is wrong, we must put up a defense to go ahead with the commission of the bad act. At the initial stage before the killing of conscience, there will be a debate for and against the action in our mind. (to do or not to do) This debate is what theology calls "temptation" - a debate before a decision is taken. If this individual succeeds in defending the reason why this bad action should be committed, the bad action is committed. Otherwise, the bad action is avoided.

Let us look at abortion through that lens as it concerns women. Take a lady, who gets pregnant. She may be a High School or College or a married lady. She knows she had sex with a man and that pregnancy could result with her action. If, at a point after the sexual intercourse, she finds out that she is pregnant, she would know that there is a baby growing inside her in some form and if she does not remove or kill the baby, after a certain number of months, she would deliver a baby and become a mother. This is a given and a reality understood by her and other adults. She does not want this to happen. So, the argument that the so-called fetus is nothing or mere tissue does not pass the test of reason. It is precisely because of this reality that another human is growing inside her, that the pregnant lady would want to do something to stop having another human being to take care of for some reasons. That is to say that if she was convinced that there was no baby in her womb, there would be no reason to panic, no reason to worry. The only reason there is panic, and worry is because she knows and every adult knows that if she did nothing about it, she would have a baby in nine months' time. So, the argument about the fetus having no life is nonsense and without merit.

Why would a woman want to abort her baby? There could be an element of fear or shame in some unmarried girls or ladies in the situation cited above. For some of the women, it could be the disruption of their education. Some of the ladies in that situation would not want the responsibility of raising a child. Some would not want to raise a child because that could tie them down and stop them from getting involved in certain other behaviors or lifestyles, they would want to be involved in. The presence of that baby would limit the lady's freedom of movement and association. To remove the shame or continue her education or maintain her freedom and lifestyle or perhaps, to continue to have sex whenever she wants, the baby in the womb has to go. This is the reality of the situation. There is no doubt that this could be a frightening experience for a woman in any of those situations. A better solution to the problem is not the denial of a life in the womb, no matter how old. But instead, the courts, politicians and abortionists deny the humanity of the baby and give him names (tissue, fetus, unwanted) to get rid of him. But another reality, and perhaps the most important, is that these "unwanted" babies or "intruders", as some people call them, did not ask to be conceived. It is generally understood that pregnancy can only happen in the context of sexual activity.

All the arguments posited above in favor of the ladies to abort their babies: removal of shame, disruption of education and limitation of lifestyle, are all selfish arguments, just for the self. But there are two lives involved in any pregnancy and nobody is thinking about the other individual who has a separate body and different DNA from the mother. Now these ladies are seeking the permission of the government and or courts to get rid of the babies. Remember that the fact that a woman is seeking permission from the government or court to get rid of a baby means that the woman knows and the government also knows that what she is asking for is a crime. What she is asking is to decriminalize a crime of abortion. That is why she is seeking permission from someone other than herself to do it. The Supreme Court of the United States of America in 1973 granted that permission and made abortion legal for all fifty States of the United States of America. The seven Justices passed a law decriminalizing abortion officially. That was a clear case of legislating from the Bench. This was when and how America lost her innocence as a nation and has not been the same ever since. Abortion was no longer a crime like adultery or murder; it was okay and official and sometimes the government pays for it at home and abroad. The journey to the bleak has just started with legal abortion.

What has happened since then is that the government has removed criminality from a crime; the Supreme Court has removed responsibility from people's bad behavior, encouraged women and their partners to carry on irresponsible sexual behaviors without consequences and passed on to the upcoming generations of young people a legacy of promiscuity, rape, no respect for life which created gang violence. This permission of the court has created confusion and conflict in the minds of young people who have been raised by their parents with religious principles and morality. The parents and the Church told them something and the court told them something else contradictory but more appealing to their lower nature. It becomes easier for the young people to reject parents and Church teaching and follow their human instincts. All this is reflected in the kind of crimes, lifestyles and value system the young generation of Americans have exhibited today. As young people this conflict is reflected in their pursuit or not of education; in their choice of partner; their decision to have children or not, their belief in God or not and the list goes on. Even when the adults who misled them pass on, they're likely to pass this tragedy onto the next generation. There lies the problem. It is easy to break a bottle; it is not easy to pick up the pieces. The latter is what we are experiencing today. How can we put the gin back in the bottle?

Young people can easily be confused and conflicted. Above we saw the **selfishness** of the women who wanted abortion. Compare the selfishness in that scenario with this next scenario. There are some children who were born with the "silver spoon" in their mouth as the saying goes. Their parents are millionaires and billionaires. These children have special treatment in the house, in the school and on the street. They get everything they want whether or not they need them. In other words, those children are raised in luxury and trained and brought up to be selfish. They do not take "no" for an answer. Since they have money, they have power and think they can get away with anything. Among this category of children, some end up getting into trouble while some do well. Among the ones who get into trouble there have been cases where their selfishness, greed and luxurious lifestyle have pushed them to kill their parents and sometimes their siblings also to be in complete control of their parents' whole estate. What do the government and courts do to these kinds of children? The government and the courts have rightly locked them up for life in prison. They lose their inheritance and their freedom as well because of their selfishness.

Now what is the difference between the selfishness of the woman who wanted sex, got pregnant and committed abortion in the first scenario and the selfishness of a young man who killed his parents to control the family estate in the second scenario? They all committed crimes. They all are adults who reasoned before their decision to follow their selfish instincts and do what they did. But one is punished by the government and the courts of America and the other is acquitted and hailed by the same government and the courts of America. To the young generation of Americans, this is confusing, conflicting and double messaging. Surprisingly America is complaining about chaos and killings in the nation. How can we expect discipline and order and respect to reign in the country which introduced violence on its own? What we reap now is exactly the fruits of what we planted through hypocrisy and injustice in 1973. That was when the government officially introduced and enthroned violence in the country but ironically is expecting discipline and peace now. The government armed her people to declare war on the unborn and turned around to preach peace while the instruments of war (abortions) are still supplied by the same government. The problems, confusion and wounds in America today are all self-made and self-inflicted. The chickens have come home to roost.

It is amazing how people in power try to stretch falsehood simply because they have the power to do so. Anyone who is genuinely looking for the truth, would always get the light of truth to solve problems such as we have here. If the Justices had genuinely asked the question about when life begins, they would have perhaps arrived at the same conclusion the other two Justices and Ms Corvey arrived at, namely that life begins at conception. Why was it difficult to accept that life begins at conception when all the ingredients that make up a person are present? God provided all that is necessary for a human being to develop. All that was left is development of the component parts already in the body. If the fetus is given time and nourishment from the mother, nature does what it does in human development, which all of us passed through. But when an adjudicator has an agenda, he/she tries to look for some other thing to fit his/her sinister desired goal. One might ask, what else is added to the fetus after conception to make it a person except time to develop - ordinarily nine months? At the moment of conception, the process of becoming a human being begins and continues unless interrupted by the violence of abortion. The so-called fetus starts to develop all the organs of the human body. It does not become any other thing but a human person like any person you see or encounter on the street. It could not become a wolf or an elephant. It could only become a human person because of the ingredients of a man's sperm and a woman's egg fused together. That fusion is called conception. That is why reasonable people say that life begins at conception. From there nature does what it does. That is how all, including abortionists and the seven justices, came to be. To say anything else is just splitting hair for the sake of argument or doing mental gymnastics.

Let us dig deeper to show that life begins at conception. Two women got pregnant the same day. Woman (A) carried her pregnancy to nine-month term and delivered a beautiful baby. But woman (B) committed abortion after four months. She claims that what was removed from her womb was not a baby but a fetus that has not become a person or baby. Now the question is: what is the difference between woman (A's) pregnancy and woman (B's) pregnancy? What exactly was added to the pregnancy of woman (A) that was missing in woman (B)? Nothing but 'Time' was missing in woman (B). If woman (B) had waited for another five months, she would have had her baby like woman (A).

The difference between woman (A) and woman (B) here is the same as the difference between the killing of a four-month-old baby outside the womb and the killing of a nine-month-old baby outside the womb. They are all babies, and they all suffered death outside the womb. But time is what puts them apart. In one case, death was common to them because they all suffered death while in the other, life or existence was not common to them because one lived for four months only while the other lived for nine months. If the person who killed the four-month-old baby had waited for five months, perhaps, they would have died the same day just as the two babies conceived the same day would, perhaps, have been born the same day if woman (B) had not committed abortion after four months. It was a question of time for nature to finish what it started in conception.

It is in the reality of this logic that HR 1997 "The Unborn Victims of Violence Act of April 1, 2004" was passed and signed into law by a Republican President George W. Bush in 2004. It passed the House by 254 to 163 and the Senate by 61 to 38 votes. This Act is a United States law that recognizes an "embryo or fetus in utero" as a legal victim if they are injured or killed during the commission of certain federal crimes of violence. Under this law, an unborn child is considered a victim because the law defines a "child in utero" as "a member of the species "Homo sapiens" at any stage of development who is carried in the womb". Emphasize the phrase "at any stage of development".

There are at least thirty-eight (38) states that have some form of "Fetal Homicide" laws in the country. Even in the liberal state of California, Mr. Scott Peterson was convicted of double homicide in the death of his pregnant wife, Laci Peterson. Yet pro-abortionists in California are doubling down on killing innocent babies in the womb because they are not "persons". The Scott Peterson double murder case exposed the double standards of liberals and abortionists especially in California. At their convenience the same baby in the womb is a human being as in the case of California v Scott Peterson and a non-human as in any abortion clinic in California depending on what is expedient. It appears that "The Unborn Victims of Violence Act of 2004" happened because there was enough 'adults' in Congress then. What a difference a few years make! Why not put selfishness, politics and commercialism aside and let children in the womb go through the same natural process every human being goes through?

The introduction of trimesters in the Roe v Wade debate is a "hail Mary" argument to try to salvage the atrocity committed by the seven Justices in Roe v Wade. I don't know if these people believed in their cause or even in God when they made that judgment. At what "mester" did God tell them that He puts a soul in the so-called fetus to become a person? Who really can answer that question? Why this "mea culpa" of restricting abortion based on trimesters' side-show, when they have already let the gin out of the bottle? With this decision the 1973 Supreme court told women: "You can kill the baby in your womb provided it is not after this trimester" or that. But why? What is it based on? What difference does it make whether you kill a man in his house or outside his house, at age twenty or thirty-six? You can as well say that one has the government's permission also to kill his child provided it is before the child reaches the age of reason, not after. No matter how you slice it, a human being is still a human being inside or outside the womb. Politicians should stop playing games with human life for political expediency. Abortion desensitizes the value of life which snowballs into indiscriminate killing of human beings everywhere in America. Abortion in the United States is a <u>United States Official Act and License</u> to kill.

<u>Congress And Abortion at Home and Overseas:</u>

Before the Supreme Court reversed Roe v Wade on June 24, 2022, Democrats in Congress had become nervous and started to make very serious and frantic moves through legislation to codify Roe v Wade before the Supreme Court gave its verdict. There was a press release on June 9, 2021, by two Democrat Senators, captioned:

Menendez and Booker to introduce bicameral legislation to guarantee equal access to abortion. "Washington D.C - U.S. Senators Bob Menendez, (D. NJ.) and Cory Booker (D. NJ) yesterday joined a group of Senate colleagues in introducing the Women's Health Protection Act (WHPA), bicameral legislation to guarantee equal access to abortion across the nation. The bill's introduction follows the Supreme Court's decision to hear arguments in a case that directly threatens 50 years of precedent protecting access to abortion and comes as states like Texas continue to pass anti-choice laws.

"It is 2021 and the fact that there are states across the country that still consider women's health a political issue instead of a human rights issue is unconscionable," said Senator Menendez. "It's time we guarantee full access to abortion for women in every city, town and state in our nation. Turning back the clock half a century is simply not an option, and I urge my colleagues to pass this bill without delay."

Joining Senator Menendez Senator Booker said:

"The repeated attacks on abortion and reproductive health care are an assault to the fundamental idea that a person's right to make their own medical decisions is an immutable, constitutional right. As these injustices threaten the rights and freedoms of all people, the Women's Health Protection Act is an important step in affirming what the Supreme Court declared decades ago, that Roe v Wade is the law of the land and that Americans have a constitutional right to make their own decisions about their bodies".

These are supposed to be adults in the room. These Democrats were so frantic that they even wrote to President Biden to use executive action to preempt the Supreme Court decision. This letter was dated June 7, 2022, and signed by 25 Democrat Senators. The letter started like this:

Dear Mr. President,

"We write to urge you to immediately issue an executive order directing the federal government to develop a national plan to defend Americans fundamental reproductive rights, including their right to an abortion…"

Senator Booker wants "Americans to have a constitutional right to make their own decisions about their bodies". I wonder if Senator Booker includes the decision of a person who wants to jump from the Empire State building or over the bridge to kill himself. Do we now allow everybody to do whatever they want to do with their body just because they want to? Why do the police and firefighters not leave individuals to jump from the bridge to death? Does he not, according to Senator Booker, have the right to kill himself since the body is his? If he does have the right over his body, why does the State, or police or firefighters intervene to stop him from jumping over the bridge or the Empire State building, Mr. Senator? If he sues the government, what will be their defense? When the Senator talks about "own bodies", is the Senator talking about the woman's body or her baby's body? Scott Peterson is sitting in prison today in liberal California State because he is convicted of double murder for killing his pregnant wife, Laci Peterson. We all know that there is a difference between the body in the womb and the body of the woman carrying the baby. There are two entities, two beings each distinct with different DNAs. So, I don't know where the woman gets the right to interfere with and kill the body of another - her baby. Senators, could you clarify those for us?

From January 22, 1973 to June 24, 2022 when the law was reversed and sent back to the States the way it was before the Norma McCorvey case, millions upon millions of children have been horribly killed by dismembering in the United States of America in the name of privacy and civil rights for pro-abortion groups. As it is now, after the June 24, 2022, decision, each state decides if abortion is legal or illegal in their state. But Democrat politicians want to fund abortion even overseas using Federal money. There is a bill now in the United States Senate called the "Abortion is Healthcare Everywhere Act". The Democrats want the killings to continue not only at home but overseas too. And they want to fund it as well with the people's money.

Since the reversal of Roe v Wade in 2022, Democrats in the House and Senate have introduced several bills to codify abortion in the American Constitution and fund abortion overseas with taxpayer money. Representative Janice Schakowsky, a Democrat from Illinois, introduced a bill in the House with 177 Democrat cosponsors to repeal the 1973 Helms Amendment that prohibited taxpayer money from being used for abortion overseas. Talking about her bill (H. R. 1670), Representative Schakowsky (D. Ill) said:

"I am proud to lead the Abortion is Health Care Everywhere Act in the House, the first-ever legislation to repeal the racist 49-year-old Helms Amendment. This harmful policy bars US Foreign Assistance from being used to offer abortion care, even in countries where abortion is legal. That is wrong. The United States should not be standing in the way of healthcare in other countries. Now, for the first time in history, this legislation is being introduced in the U.S Senate. I am grateful for Senator Booker's leadership to repeal the Helms Amendment and expand abortion access in this critical moment. Abortion is healthcare and healthcare is a human right."

In the Senate, Senator Cory Booker, a Democrat Senator from Jew Jersey on July 27, 2022, introduced a bill (S.B.929) to repeal the 1973 Helms Amendment, which prevented taxpayer money from being used for abortion overseas. Senator Booker had 24 Democrat cosponsors for this bill. In his speech Senator Booker said:

"We know that in the wake of Dobbs v Jackson Women's Health, Americans will be denied access to essential health care services across the United States; however, the repercussions also go beyond our borders. This disastrous decision will be felt around the world, setting back many countries who have long used Roe v Wade as the basis to strengthen abortion rights protections in their own countries. We must take immediate action to mitigate the global impact of this decision. For this reason, I am proud to introduce the Abortion is Health Care Everywhere

Act, which will repeal the Helms Amendment and ensure that U.S. foreign assistance can be used for safe abortion services overseas."

About S.B. 929, one of the cosponsors, Senator Hirono, a Democrat from Hawaii said:

"The fight to secure reproductive health care for all does not stop at our borders. By ending the prohibition on foreign aid being used for safe abortion care, the Abortion is Health Care Everywhere Act will help expand access to critical reproductive services in some of the world's most vulnerable communities. As we fight to defend fundamental reproductive rights in the U.S., this legislation will help millions around the world exercise their right to access comprehensive reproductive health care services."

This is how the Democrats we sent to Washington D. C. are using their power to introduce to our young people a culture of death. Look at what Senator Hirono said again:

"As we fight to defend fundamental reproductive rights in the U.S., this legislation will help millions around the world exercise their right to access comprehensive reproductive health care services."

The Senator from Hawaii used the term "reproductive health care services", which leaves one to scratch his head to ask: what is "reproductive health care services" in killing a baby in the womb? There is no healthcare service in killing. Here again we have adults behaving recklessly and introducing recklessness to young people. Young people learn fast especially when it comes from adults in authority. That is why streets in America are ridden with rival gang violence, chaos and deaths, which are just an extension of the violence of abortion introduced to them by their Democrat politicians and mentors in Washington D.C. But ironically the same people somehow expect a culture of life and peace to reign in the nation of violence. How do you do that?

Preservation of life, liberty and the pursuit of happiness in the First Amendment was totally forgotten by the seven Justices in Roe v Wade in 1973 and these Democrat politicians. Today the pro-abortionists and these politicians are still not getting it that the preservation of life, liberty and the pursuit of happiness should be the right of all Americans "in or extra utero". In like manner abortion doctors forgot their "Hippocratic oath" to preserve and protect life to make money. What used to be an offense prosecutable under the law is no longer an offense. People went to prison for killing, cheating, stealing, perjury etc. But the Supreme Court made a distinction between killing a baby in the womb and killing a baby outside the womb. Killing a baby outside the womb is murder; but inside the womb, it is abortion and therefore is legal. Ridiculous!

Unfortunately, the number of children, who died through abortion in the United States of America, do not include the millions of children killed in the womb worldwide through abortion with money from the United States of America through the auspices of different American Foundations like John D. Rockefeller and Bill Gates, Melinda French Gates and George Soros' Open Society Foundation and other government funds. These Foundations and Planned Parenthood believe that the world is full now since they themselves are already in the world. It is like the "one child" policy in China, a practice America has been fighting to stop in the name of Freedom. Most of the abortion killings overseas which are couched in financial aids and benevolence, were done in unsuspecting African and South American countries. Ironically the billions of dollars America used to abort babies in Africa and other third world countries would be more than enough to feed those babies and more. America used to go to other countries to save lives. But now they do not only kill babies at home; they do the same abroad. It was not enough for them that millions of children have died through abortion in the United States of America; they use their Foundations and taxpayer money to spread the culture of death by killing babies worldwide in the name of international aid and what they now call "healthcare services" for women.

CHAPTER TEN: THE REMOTE SIDE EFFECTS OF ORGANIZED ABORTIONS ON AMERICAN SOCIETY

Abortion is not a new phenomenon in the world or in America. Like other natural crimes, abortion has been around for a while. Cain killed his brother, Abel in the Old Testament. The disordered nature of humans carries with it disordered effects like murder, cheating, lying, raping, stealing and destruction of other people's valuables and of course, abortion. That is precisely why God gave humanity laws to follow to peacefully coexist with one other in society. In any society people come together to make specific laws based on the laws God laid down for humanity. Laws make for good understanding, peace and harmony between people. They are like "barriers", "walls" or "fences" between neighbors. They "make for good neighbors", to quote Robert Frost's poem, "Mending Wall". They make for peace. If there are no walls between neighbors, fights might ensue and there might be no peace between those neighbors. When people infringe on these laws made by God, the infringement fractures society. That is why society imposes punishment to offer a sort of deterrent. With punishment people learn from their mistakes and society functions better and more peacefully.

But when society slackens the enforcement of the laws they have made, bad actors get emboldened and commit more offenses and society deteriorates even further. When America legalized abortion in the country, it carried with it certain negative consequences. The first blow to morality and human decency in America was the exposure of young people to casual sex as a form of exercise in freedom. Free sex and cohabitation of young people became casual, more frequent and normal since there is no consequence for those actions. The clinics are there to take care of any subsequent pregnancies, thanks to abortion and the adults in the room.

That reinforced the sexual revolution of the sixties. We know that students and the unmarried, who are constantly experimenting on sex without thinking of the consequences of their actions, became the most promiscuous in American history. And as always, such actions have their own consequences. Incidents of so-called "unwanted pregnancies" explode. Since there are no deterrents to abortion, pregnancies increase followed by more abortions. As a result of that, more babies are killed every day of the week. The more these young people procure abortions, the more desensitized they become to disposing of human life, not only in having more abortions, but in street killings by gang rivals. If one factors in the fact that pro-abortion groups have avenues of raising money to pay for abortion for people, who are poor or indigent students, more and more abortions take place with impunity. After all, it is all free. As if that was not bad enough, taxpayer funds are sometimes used to pay for abortion in minority communities directly or indirectly. In America the reality is that there are more abortions in poor neighborhoods than rich neighborhoods. We are all familiar with how free stuff works among poor people.

We are all aware of the damage the welfare system did in minority communities in America. Those minority neighborhoods are still suffering from the scars of unmitigated welfarism of the seventies and eighties. When the welfare system was introduced in this country, it was to give a temporary helping hand to poor blacks and Hispanics who had a misfortune in the family or some other temporary situation to get back their independence once more. But it was hijacked by politicians as an instrument of using government money to get minority votes in elections. By using this tactic to stay in power, the welfare system became a permanent structure that ruined poor communities across America. That was and still is how the Democrats solidified their hold on black Americans for their votes till today. They give them free government money for their unalloyed votes and allegiance. That is why President Biden told a black American: "if you have to think if you should vote for me or Trump, you aren't black." The monthly checks, food stamps and government High rises in the poor neighborhoods as free accommodation, finally took away the independence of these minorities to be free to go as far on the ladder of success as possible. That freedom would liberate them from politicians who would like to think for them what was best for them.

What more devastating help can the government give to a man, who receives a welfare check, food stamps and free accommodation in a high rise every month doing nothing? Meanwhile his two sons with their children and two unmarried daughters are there with their children in the High rise under the same government freebie. For generation after generation, such people's economic growth and or awareness is permanently blocked or stunted. Just imagine the damage these politicians have done to the pride and dignity of these black people. These able-bodied men and women found time to dabble into doing and selling drugs to the younger generation. Over the years the damage becomes irreparable. The greedy politicians want to make these poor people dependent on the Government to make sure they have their votes come the next election which keeps them in power. But the unfortunate result is that the Government has shut down the psychological, mental and personal growth of parents, children and grandchildren of High-rise dwellers. That was, of course, the beginning of the problems of the American poor neighborhoods of today where abortions, drugs and other crimes abound. A political party used the welfare system and free abortion to poor women to hold generations of minorities hostage in their own country. It is an unfair control of a segment of the population because politicians want to run the lives of poor people perpetually by taxing and blowing the Federal deficits whenever they are in power to give free money to their hostages to keep them quiet and loyal. In the meantime, abortion is highest in these neighborhoods because it is free and young people have a lot of time on their hands. The young people in these neighborhoods give up education for drugs, sex and gang activities. The welfare and other freebies are the origin of how black America got married to the Democrat party. Until recently no blacks voted Republican. No wonder it has earned any black Americans voting Republican the nickname, "sell-out".

The freer abortion is available, the more the moral standards in these demographics deteriorate. Young girls do not have any qualms or shame frequenting abortion clinics just as habitual criminals, frequent prisons without regrets or shame. The people who, in my opinion, engage in these criminal activities, become desensitized to killing inside and outside the womb. Frequenting abortion clinics and or going to prison become casual and normal in these neighborhoods. As they say: "once you have killed before it becomes easier to kill again and again". Abortion becomes the enabler of armed robbery and gang shootings in so many cities, especially those run by the same party that doles out government freebies. After all these young men and women in the gangs are involved and are part of the abortion too. It becomes commonplace for armed robbers to go to anybody's house, rob and kill the occupants of the house or bank if there is any resistance. For them it is only shooting and killing people who have all the wealth of the nation; so, what? They have done it so many times before just as they have enabled and participated in so many governments sponsored abortions before. For such individuals, life becomes so cheap that they have no feelings disposing of it. To kill becomes fun as in a game of sports. The frequency of killing babies in the womb without feelings, remorse or accountability has developed into killing of people outside the womb without any feelings, thanks to politicians and the courts, which condoned abortion.

It is amazing how taking away somebody's life is nothing to several of the present generation of young people who constitute themselves into gangs - blacks killing blacks; Hispanics killing Hispanics. The failure and selfishness of politicians are, of course, what created the gang culture. These are frustrated children who want to belong to a meaningful structure. Since the system denies them that, they make their own structure and rules, which they police vigorously. Belonging to a gang group gives them meaning, power and structure. They police their own and respect hierarchy and surprisingly, discipline. Killing a subordinate in a flash is common to teach others a lesson. But the philosophy of each gang group is to out-do and out-shine the other as well as maintain power. That mentality drives them to kill mercilessly. As part of initiation a gang member has got to brutally and callously kill someone to the cheers and admiration of some other gang members as witnesses. Then and only then is he/she regarded as a full member of the group. Now I ask, America, how did we get here? No more sympathy! No more feelings! Just take a gun and possess the appetite to kill! It is like a lady going to an abortion clinic to kill the baby in her womb. It is the same feeling abortionists have when they perform abortions. There are no feelings and at the end of the day, they go home happily satisfied that they have done their job for the day. Next day they go back to kill more babies. As for the lady, she goes home happy that her obstacle is out of the way and that makes her happy and ready in a few months' time to repeat the process. The government is on her side and the law is on her side, thanks to the 1973 Supreme Court decision.

There is a gang shootout and drive-by shootings every day in many cities like Chicago, Detroit, Los Angeles, Oakland, San Francisco, Baltimore, Sacramento, Seattle, Philadelphia, Stockton, Portland, Ontario and Washington DC with many casualties. What is common to these cities? They are run by Democrat Mayors who don't like the Second Amendment, and they ban guns in their cities. But who says that criminals obey laws? It is only the law-abiding citizens who obey these gun laws and are disarmed. When the criminals show up on their doorsteps with guns, they become helpless. But meanwhile the lawmakers have bodyguards, who protect them from their own bad laws. Flip the page to a Republican city where the Second Amendment is in force. The criminals do not show up on people's doorsteps easily because they know that the house owner is probably armed and ready to defend his house and family. That is how Republican cities are relatively calm. But unfortunately, unnecessary spilling of human blood everyday becomes a normal occurrence all over the cities that have strict gun laws. Some politicians put the blame on the proliferation of guns. Of course, they will not put the blame on what caused the young men and women to devalue life through abortion. Politicians will not take the blame on how they supported the killing of innocent babies in the womb. That would make them feel guilty. Instead, they shift the blame on guns. But how is it that the states and cities that have the strongest gun laws and controls in the country also have the worst shootings and worst loss of lives through abortion and gang rivalries, bank robberies and other senseless killings? How is it that the states which have strict abortion laws and respect for the Second Amendment have less killings by far? Guns don't kill people; people kill people with guns. The gun does not shoot by itself. Good and sane people, who own guns, don't shoot people. It is estimated that about 82.8 million people in America own guns. Most of these millions of gun owners are law abiding Americans, who don't go about killing people. So, it is not the guns that kill people; bad people kill people. And these people kill because they have no respect for life and no respect for the Author of life, God. What criminals and mentally deranged people use to kill is accidental because they could use any other instrument other than guns. People are killed by poison, with knives, baseball bats or by strangling. Should we ban knives and baseball bats because bad people use them to kill others? If abortion is still legal and there are no guns in America, those who are prone to kill, will still kill by other means because life doesn't mean anything to them. It is the formation of individual character and their relationship with the Creator that determines whether they will harm other people, not the instrument used. Irresponsibility breeds irresponsibility. Government approval of violence on the unborn breeds violence in that society. And it is all about power over weakness. When the courts or politicians approve of irresponsible sexual behaviors which bring about abortion, other irresponsible behaviors like gang and random killings, alcohol and drugs naturally follow. To get rid of the subsequent bad behaviors on our streets today, it will be better to start to dismantle the original bad behaviors endorsed by the government.

CHAPTER ELEVEN: THE COLLAPSE OF THE AMERICAN FAMILY

The family is the nucleus of society. Every society, every nation is made up of families. One can accurately say that the success of the family is the success of the society. The health and sanity of the family translates into the health and sanity of society. It is also true that the failure of the family is also the failure of society. If God governs every family in society, automatically God will govern the entire society. Expel God in the family, there will be no God in that society and chaos will reign. This basic principle has been true in the history of man all the time in every case. The surest way to destroy a country is to destroy the families in that country. The devil knows that very well and is systematically using atheists in our society in the camouflage of progressivism and liberalism to accomplish that goal of destroying the family and subsequently the nation. This plot to destroy the family has been in progress for a while now in America. The effect of that plot is manifesting itself now. What is happening to the United States of America today must be traced back to the collapse of the American family in the sixties when the bizarre and the abnormal were introduced to America as normal.

Children are the future of any society. The formative years of children are crucial to their future and the future of that society. The ideal structure of a family is one with children and two parents. I say two parents because one parent or more than two parents is the beginning of problems for the family and ultimately the society. While the former (one parent family) is a European and American problem, the latter (more than two parents) is an African problem. We dealt with the latter in another topic - polygamy. In America today there is an increase in fatherless homes. In a fatherless home, we only have a mother to take care of the children by playing the role of a mother and a father at the same time. Realistically we know that a woman cannot play the role of a man in the house adequately nor can a man play the role of a woman adequately either. Consequently, something is going to give in, especially with the boys in the family. While there have been few instances where the children of a one parent family have come out fine, children are better off with two parents. In the case of the death of one of the parents, there isn't much anybody can do about that. In fact, among the one parent families where one of the spouses passes away, many of the children do very well. Both the remaining spouse and the children face the challenge of death together squarely. Their circumstances bond them together and make them more sympathetic and caring people. They learn the lessons and challenges of life together and early and become determined to succeed. The children's anger is placed on death, not the surviving parent or society. They are determined to help the surviving parent to make the family a success. Where we have the greatest family problem in a single parent family is when two adults get children into the world and chicken-out through divorce, which most of the time is out of their selfishness. They think about themselves only without any consideration of the children. That is why many times the children start acting out in rebellion and end up with the wrong crowds.

When divorce happens, the children by law stay with the woman unless in some extreme circumstances when the woman has other problems. We know that child support is not always enough or forthcoming. In some cases, the mother's income will barely be enough to take care of the household. That in effect will make the woman take two or three jobs to put a roof over their heads, clothes on their backs and food on the table. While the woman is busy doing two or three jobs, the children have little or no supervision at home because there is no man in the house while the woman is doing two jobs. The children invariably lose the benefits of proper parenting in those critical years of their lives. Once the reality of two parent care is lost in a family, there is no way the affected children will go back as adults to capture those lost treasures. They are gone and the negative effects will remain with the children as well as their own future family and society at large unless there is some strong intervention later. Whenever there are no parents at home, children naturally tend to become their own parents. They educate themselves in whatever way they can. Naturally they must deal with whatever obstacles and bad influences they encounter in school and after school with their peers. Children in such situations, boys and girls, end up trying things out to fill up the void. They may latch on to the bad habits of some older children in their circles. They may inevitably experiment on smoking, drugs and sex. Older school mates may engage the younger ones in running drug operations for some change in their pockets. As they increase their interest in these bad habits, they lose interest in their academic pursuit and drop out of school before they even know it. Meanwhile the mother is spending more hours at work than at home and nobody is looking into their schoolwork. In some cases, the mother of the house finds out that there is a problem in the house only when one of the boys is arrested by the police on drug possession or one of the girls is pregnant. Such a situation puts the woman in a double jeopardy stance with an attendant guilt. She is presented with a "to be or not to be" question. That is single parenthood in practice.

Unfortunately, the government is not helping the situation by the type of laws they pass and promulgate in welfare cases where they penalize a welfare recipient who does some extra job to augment the welfare payout. If the welfare recipients were allowed to work part time, that in effect, would help the recipient to make enough money for the family and still supervise the children or perhaps get a better apartment in a better neighborhood. When the welfare check is not enough for the family and the welfare recipient is not allowed to do extra work, the recipient is forced to get out of welfare and take multiple jobs at the detriment of the children's supervision. In the interest of our children, this is an area that politicians should investigate to help children where the father is absent and not fulfilling his financial obligations. Though the absence of a father in a home is irreplaceable, this welfare law adjustment could only be the second-best thing in the situation, which has the potential of at least redeeming some of the children in this situation in the future.

Whenever there are a couple of students, who have tasted indiscipline at home amid other students, there is bound to be a trans-contamination of bad behavior to the student body. It will not take long before the school authorities realize they have, for instance, a drug problem and indiscipline in their school. It takes only a few problematic students in the school to institute a drug problem in a school. The devastating effect of this scenario is the lowering of academic standards, drug addiction, mental illness and sometimes death through overdose or suicide. Where did all this start from? In homes without fathers! A troublesome child comes to school with all the family baggage, and it spreads throughout the school. One bad student can and does have negative effects on a large portion of the student population. According to Pew Research Center:

"Two parent households are on the decline in the United States as divorce, remarriage and cohabitation are on the rise".

There you have it from Pew Research Center. This increase in the number of cohabitations, divorce and remarriage was the product of the lifestyles of the sixties. The introduction of excessive alcohol consumption and drugs in the sixties brought about free and irresponsible sexual activities, which produced children out of wedlock or created bad marriages entered without full knowledge. In a lot of cases, out of wedlock children are raised by the mothers alone or the grandmothers and the cycle is replicated. In some cases, the children know their fathers but in most of the cases, the children have no idea who their fathers are. In this category of children, their fathers have probably five or six other children with five or six other women. (sexual revolution!) More than half of these men are in and out of prison. Each time they come out of prison, they father some more children and go back to the prison because of their lifestyle of drugs, alcoholism, rape, stealing or murder. The prison is their home, their comfort zone, a place where they escape from responsibility. Everything is paid for by the taxpayer. If we average three or four children per such men in and out of prison, how many children are we talking about at risk in the nation? Millions! This lifestyle tends to create men who think they have some entitlement to things they want. They don't like school or working to earn a living. But they have their eyes on other people's hard-earned money. They are quick to complain about people who have too much money. It is the same kind of men that rape women as part of that "right" and "entitlement". Unfortunately, some rapists also kill their victims.

On the other hand, what kind of girls or ladies hang around boys and men like that? Birds of the same feather, they say, flock together. School dropouts, promiscuous, no sex boundary people, drug and alcohol abusers tend to hang out and drink or do drugs together. That is when things get out of hand and things happen. The culture of responsibility is dead to people of this nature, thanks to our political leaders and adults in the room who created that environment. It is also a known fact that some of these women do not want any man in the house, anyway. For this type of girls or women, a man in the house is a check on their freedom. Selfishness is still at work in such women. They know where their men are while their men don't know where they are because the men are in prison. They have the advantage over the men and many times the women don't even know who the father of their children is because they have sex with multiple men at the same time. All they want from the men are the children to increase their welfare check at the end of the month. According to the welfare law, the more children, the more welfare checks! For these women it is the money; it is not the men, and it is not even the children that they are interested in. In some cases, these checks don't even go for the welfare of the children, but for whatever the woman is addicted to. How can a woman like that give good direction to the children? That is a big attack on the traditional family. Very often these habits rub off on the children and society suffers for it as always. Where is the government in all this? It was the government which kicked off the wrong ball rolling and the chickens have come home to roost. These manifestations of family breakdown started with the sexual revolution; that was when young people declared their "freedom", left the home to live out their kind of lifestyle in cohabitation, immorality and drugs.

According to Pew Research Center, after World War 11, "73% of all children were living in a family with two married parents in their first marriage. By 1980, 61% of children were living in this type of family and today less than half (46%) are". Children living with single and cohabiting parents have changed the American family landscape.

This revolution in family structure has its own resultant negative effects for families and society at large. In an article written by Jason Wise titled: Fatherless Homes Statistics 2023, Risks and Repercussions: he highlighted several negative statistics concerning children raised in fatherless homes, which is the result of divorce, remarriage and cohabitation of married and unmarried couples. He observed that the

2021 US Census Bureau reported that 18.4 million children live in homes without a father and that such children are four times more likely to live below poverty level. There are also homes without mothers. This is a situation where mothers abandon their children and run off with another man or they are so far gone with doing drugs and alcohol that they could not take care of themselves let alone their children. This research also shows 1.8 million children are living in homes with their fathers without their mothers. According to his research, "children of fatherless households are two times more likely to drop out of school."

In such homes there is likely no discipline in the home. The children grow up faster than their age and become streetwise very fast and too early. The woman of the house is rarely at home to help with their schoolwork because she is doing two and sometimes three jobs to make ends meet. Some such women are addicted to alcohol or drugs and have no time for the children. Sooner or later, going to school becomes boring for the children and they drop out to make fast money in the lucrative drug business or join the gang for recognition, fellowship and empowerment which they do not get at home.

The boyfriend of their mother sleeps in the house and they know he is not their father. What goes on in the house between him and their mother becomes a moral issue for developing minds. Resentment sets in and becomes a serious issue for the children later in life. The children in this situation tend to use bad language, cultivate revolting behaviors and anti-social outbursts at home and outside the home. Before they are of age, the boys and girls take their moral cue from their lived experience in the house. With the immoral situation in the home, neither the mother nor the live-in boyfriend has the courage to correct or steer the children right because they could not be role models to the children by their own lifestyle. The children become sexually active at a very early age. Even in the case of the household where there is only the father present, there is very often another kind of problem. Invariably the father will have a live-in girlfriend, who would claim to be the woman of the house. In ninety nine percent of the time, the man's children do not recognize the "live-in mom" and will not obey her. The resultant revolt will scatter the children because their father will most of the time side with his girlfriend and some of the children would run away from the home to fend for themselves. The girls may end up with prostitution. And it is rough out there and they could become victims of homicide. Gang-banging, teen pregnancies and repeat abortions will become a frequent occurrence which subsequently impacts American families and society.

The research shows that "teen pregnancy rates are higher in fatherless homes" than in two parent households. Ordinarily the man has a unique role in the house that a woman could not play. So, when he is absent, it creates some behavioral problems in the household. According to these statistics, "studies show that children of fatherless homes, or homes where the father is disengaged, are more likely to develop behavioral problems." Also "adolescents from fatherless homes are more likely to commit crimes". When Teens run away from home, crimes become the next best thing for survival on the street. That is why the Federal Bureau of prisons statistics show that 85% of prisoners are from fatherless homes. But in the State Prisons the figure is 70% of the prisoners. The same study found that 57.6 % of African American children have absent fathers and 72.2 % of Americans believe that fatherless homes are the biggest social problem in the country. Without a doubt most of the ills of American society are because of the collapse of the American family.

According to these statistics among children unhoused and runaways in America, 90% came from fatherless households while 80% of all rapists with anger issues were raised in fatherless households. Fatherless household statistics reveal that 70% of America's youths that are living in State-run Institutions are from fatherless households. 90% of repeat offender teen arsonists were raised in fatherless households. In almost all these situations it can be noticed that anger issues are very common. The children feel abandoned and neglected and they start to act out their anger and frustration in arson, rape and other deviant behaviors and addictions. Those numbers tell a very ominous story of the situation in America. It tells why America has so many men and women incarcerated. But why are politicians not looking at the problem of fatherless homes in America? The answer is obvious. A lot of the politicians are the cause of the problem of fatherless homes. It all started with permissiveness, the anything goes mentality in the guise of "freedom", then divorce, the free sex without responsibility and the expulsion of God from schools.

Children in Private and Church schools don't have these problems because there is God and discipline in school. Some of the politicians are sponsored by atheist millionaires and billionaires who want the family structures destroyed. If the family is destroyed, things will never be the same again. That is how we landed where we are now.

There is another attitude that has severely contributed negatively to the decay of the American family and society. That is the current nonchalant attitude of Americans toward marriage. This lack of respect for marriage springs from the overall attitude of the people toward God, the Author of marriage. When people, as a culture, lose respect for marriage as an institution, Democrat politicians, campaign and encourage "free sex" and abortion, it devalues and belittles marriage. When same sex marriage is recognized, by government, it cuts into the respect for marriage. To several Americans today, marriage is like a joke. It carries no weight, and it can be dissolved any time for any reason. A lot of American young people today do not want to get married in the Church because that might evoke some seriousness and dignity to marriage. The sense of the sacred and awe scares young people who don't want marriage to be a lasting experience. Instead, they prefer to marry on the beach, in a garden or skydiving. They will exchange vows anywhere devoid of seriousness or sacredness. In short, they don't want God in it because they are not sure of where the marriage will go since about fifty percent of all marriages in America end up in divorce. They have no Faith in it. Consider this; 29 States allow pets to be official witnesses in couples' weddings. Even 8 of the States allow pets to officiate at weddings instead of a human being - clergy person or State official. How serious could such a wedding be? Sacramental? Seriously? Of God? Of course not! People who make these laws belittle marriage and it is a shame. Some people don't see the institution of marriage as something of God. It becomes principally a "sex thing". In that situation the union of a man and a woman becomes merely casual and can be dismantled at will any time. The so-called relationship is built only on sex or dominion one over the other. That takes respect out of a relationship as it should be. This attitude brings about divorce in an institution of marriage which was meant for permanency. When that permanence is removed, it fractures both the children and the family itself; and the society is also fractured.

As we have seen, the removal of God in American schools and largely the American life, affects every other thing that we do as human beings in this system. It is at that point that selfish nature takes over and makes it close to impossible, at least in the mind, for a man and a woman to live together in an institution called marriage. When divorce takes place, children are permanently scarred both in their present family and their future families and the result is shown in the value and quality of life in those affected. The adverse product of the destruction of marriage and family is seen every day on the streets of America.

How did America get to this point? What percentage of Americans today believe that children are intrinsically part of marriage as an institution? Many of the latest generations of **X Y** and **Z** do not seem to see children as part of marriage. It is weird to even think about. It is very common these days to see couples living together without any desire to have children. What happened to "increase and multiply" in the Bible? They only see their relationship as a sexual engagement because contraceptives and abortion are there to cover them and remove any personal responsibility. They get married only to express themselves in sexual activities, nothing more. That is one group. There is another group which does not go through any marriage ceremonies at all, but they live together for sexual gratification. Their selfish nature does not want any responsibility for taking care of children. They have and enjoy good homes and lavish lifestyles. Their association is built on self and when the self is no longer gratified, it is time to split. Each ego is on its way out of the relationship reinforced with a sense of self-righteousness. The same scenario is played repeatedly as many times as possible. Sacrifice, which is the engine house and success of any marriage, family and nation, is lost forever on people like these. Unfortunately, this shelving of responsibility on the part of some elements of gens- XYZ, seems to contribute to the number of young people who believe they are gays or bisexual. They hate the idea of raising children.

The attitude described above started about fifty years ago. Before then American families were large. The average number of children in a family then was about five or six. Contraceptives and abortion were not popular then. The average number of children today in the American family is 2.7 children. Selfishness was not as glamorous then as it is today because responsibility and selflessness were part and parcel of the family then. Everyone in the family unit was looking outward for the good of all the members of the family and food and amenities were shared cheerfully. So here we are in a nation where a big chunk of her population wants to cohabit for sexual gratification only or some who want to get married without children and of those who agree to have children, two children is the maximum per family. The .7 children per family in the statistics is only there because of Mexican and Muslim immigrants and a few Catholics, who believe that children come from God and should be welcomed. That makes up for those who don't want any children. The older Hispanics and Muslims also believe that if their own parents sacrificed for them to exist, they were willing to sacrifice for their own children. That is for the good and survival of the nation and the human species. The 2.7 children per American family today will definitely get worse as the young population increases and the gay and transgenderism progress as the years go by. We are now complaining about how 'Social Security' is in danger of collapse because there are not enough people in the middle to contribute to pay the current recipients, wait till the generations XYZ step up the social security ladder. That is why it is scary to see where America is consciously and deliberately going. Scarry! It doesn't look good.

CHAPTER TWELVE: THE POLITICIANS' COMPLICITY IN THE YOUTH DELINQUENCY

American youths seem to be off the charts in crimes and other societal ills that have changed the face of America recently. Accomplice in this tragedy of lawlessness in the country is pointing to the ruling class, the politicians and "legislative courts" (courts that make laws). Politics is a very strong force in American society. It is the politicians who make and enforce laws in the country. As we noted earlier the courts and the politicians removed God from the school system. The attorneys took the law and ran with it to an even more ridiculous position just to make money. Bad political decisions, over the years, have negatively affected the behavior of many generations of Americans. It has contributed to all kinds of delinquencies in minors who have grown up to constitute problems and not only become liabilities in society today, but they have brought into the world people like themselves who constitute problems as well. The absence of God in the formative years of American children develops into some crises during teen years and lingers on and matures in later years to affect even their own children. The cycle of decadence continues. Teen delinquencies and crimes, drug use, alcoholism, school dropouts, gang violence, school shootings, depression, suicide, mental disorders, rape and other sex crimes, teen and single parenthood, disregard for human life, homelessness and indiscriminate murder in and outside the womb are manifestations of a life without grace and God. Not every child has a two-parent household to help them fend off the effects of these adult-imposed obstacles in a child's development journey. Some of these parents have already been cut up on this web and are not in the position to help the children they have brought into the world. Such children have no fighting chance at all, and they are sucked into a societal mess that is not of their making and the tragedy continues in their own offspring for future generations. Sooner or later, some of these people find themselves through elections in the corridors of power with all that baggage. As we know, elections are a game of numbers and money. When we have enough members of questionable character in a community, they will likely vote one of their kind in a position of power. That could start the ball rolling. With this complication, it becomes difficult to turn things around later when some sanity shows up in that community. Instead, new abnormalities emerge. This results in having Godless and irresponsible members of congress making laws for the nation. That is the story of America today.

How do politicians influence society, one might ask? They make the laws and execute the laws. They also elect or confirm the judges, who interpret the laws that govern the people. In an official way, only the President and the lawmakers are referred to as politicians but in a loose sense all the three branches of government now seem to be politicians, as has been revealed of late. It is not a hidden fact that there are many judges who legislate from the bench instead of interpreting the laws. These kinds of Judges rule on what they think the law should have been, not what the lawmakers have written down. This is how some of the judges have become part of the political problem. A real and good judge interprets the law as it is written without bias or sentiments on how it affects the subjects, no matter how badly. This is precisely why judges are not normally regarded as politicians because they are supposed to be neutral umpires in interpreting what the law says irrespective of whom they think the law should favor. The job of the judiciary is not what the law should have been, but what it is as written. The intentionality of that area of the law is the job of the one who made the law. The lawmakers have some intention when they craft the law/s. When the interpretation reveals an unintended consequence, the lawmaker can revisit and amend the law. This adjustment is not the job of the bench. That was how it was designed to be by the Founding Fathers until partisanship and division in society affected the members of the bench, who became loyal to the party that appointed them or the electorate that elected them in some cases. As it is now, every branch is fighting for its own and its survival. Unfortunately, the Judiciary is not left out in this partisanship. On their own each political party is fighting hard to get representatives in the judiciary for the unfortunate reason, which is destroying America even more.

In some parts of the country, elected District Attorneys (DAs), make criminals, victims and the real victims, criminals, to please the people who elected them. What can anyone do about it, since the DAs are the ones, the law gives the right to prosecute or not to prosecute a case? In other words, a District Attorney (DA) can set a criminal free and that is the end of the case. When the politicians make laws that are criminals friendly and there is a District Attorney that is criminals friendly, criminals are emboldened to go out to commit more and more crimes with impunity and the community is not only terrorized but degraded more and more. That sets off a trend of crimes and violence in that society and the young criminals learn fast to congregate in a "welcoming" community to operate freely. It does not take rocket science to know this. Young people need adult direction and supervision to mold good characters who eventually become good citizens. But when adults relinquish their responsibility for "playing politics", they create a situation where "the inmates run the asylum". That is how politicians can create criminals out of our children. Then everybody will start to blame the young people. But it is the adults and the political class that is responsible for the delinquency of young people.

It starts, for instance, when a city council or State legislators or liberal voters put in place a law that encourages young people to steal. In California, for instance, proposition 47 said that petty theft should be treated as misdemeanor. It goes to define petty theft as "obtaining any property by theft where the value of the money, labor, real or personal property taken" does not exceed $950.00. If a person steals or loots material from a store worth $950.00, that person would not go to prison for it. What does that kind of law tell young people? Are the legislators expecting a crime-free city and state with a law like that? Unfortunately, progressives and liberals think that they are helping these young people by not punishing them. What do they expect the young criminals in the city and state to do? They will, of course, declare war on all the stores in the area. The politicians have failed these youths by not creating jobs for them and now they make a law to give them a break if they steal. In those Democrat Cities and States that have such ridiculous laws, we have seen an explosion of lawlessness. There have been cases where a group of young people of about twenty or more would go into one store in the area at a time and loot on a regular basis and nothing will happen to them by way of prison term. If this is done every week, what will happen to the stores in the city? What becomes the fate of the owners of these stores that are looted daily or weekly? The business owners leave the city for good. This is how a once prospering city gets to become a run-down city because of "very wise and sympathetic progressives", who want to be "sympathetic" to the "poor" people they created in the first place by the stupid laws they made. The liberal and progressive politicians make these stupid laws to compensate for the lack of jobs for young people and their families, whom they need their votes to stay in power. They end up ruining their city and state because the money-makers and law-abiding inhabitants leave the city and state for good as well. What are they left with? More crimes, graffiti and run down cities which are infested with crimes, drug addicts and homelessness! Then the politicians will tax the poor people left in the city to rebuild the city which they destroyed. Adults make criminals out of young people by stupid laws they make.

It is the adults elected by the people who empower young people to a life of drugs by decriminalizing drugs. When politicians go from decriminalizing marijuana and young marijuana users graduate to a more potent and addictive drug and get addicted, it is the same politicians and city council members or state legislators who make another law to issue "clean needles" to drug addicts to prevent the addicts from getting infected with HIV. What was a stupid law like that supposed to do for the drug addict? But one would think that city council members would know that giving clean needles to drug addicts would increase the number of addicts in the city and even import more addicts from other cities. To the addicts, clean needles become one thing they don't have to worry about to keep the habit. It is the politicians who legalized marijuana, the gate-way drug for recreational use in many Democrat States like California that opened the way for hard drugs and drug addiction. What is that all about? How does that help society? These politicians create the problem, scandalize the young people and they go ahead to exacerbate the problem they created. What a way to go! Putting a fox in charge of the chicken house for safety!

No child is born a monster. No child is born a criminal. In most cases criminals are made by adults in their lives and environments. We have seen how sets of politicians create monsters who terrorize the city and make it uninhabitable. The so-called "poor" people and the drug addicted people they claim to help with stupid laws happen to be the products of their policies and political ambitions. These same "poor" people end up suffering from the effects of the bad laws and policies that politicians have made. When the store owners and law-abiding citizens desert the city, it is the same "poor" people, whom the politicians say they are protecting, who will remain in the rundown city to bear the brunt of the disaster because they cannot relocate to better neighborhoods for obvious reasons. Where is the wisdom of such policies and politicians who create problems that leave the city or state worse than when they came into office? When we replicate the one city scenario to many other badly run cities in the nation, we have a nation in need of a Savior. That seems to be where we are now under Biden.

The way some politicians manage the schools is of course, the reason many of the students drop out of school and start the dangerous journey to criminality. Surprise? Who runs the schools and who are the members of the School Boards which hire those who train these children? They are politicians. It will be interesting to know what their agenda is. Many school districts devote a reasonable sum of the taxpayers' money for the education of the young people. But the results are not commensurate with the amount spent to educate the children. Money is spent but there are no good results. Why is that? Everything depends on the board that administers the schools in the area. Their priorities matter a lot. In a lot of cases, their priorities are not to produce well rounded, educated students, who will be the future of the community and the country. Their priority is their politics at the expense of the students. If fraternizing with the parents and students with their wishy-washy laws will mean easy reelection for them, then that will become their priority. Then a policy is formulated to reflect that priority. They will craft the laws accordingly to achieve that goal. It is all politics. State legislatures make laws that govern the conduct of school administrators, teachers and students. They also formulate disciplinary measures for everyone in the school system to make sure administrators, teachers and students don't step outside their boundaries. There are some actions by students that would warrant a suspension for days or weeks depending on the seriousness of the offense to teach them discipline. Such laws are supposed to help mold the character of the young people who need help to become good citizens in the future. But some politicians do only what is to their political advantage.

Now watch this. The California legislature, for instance, has passed a law amending the existing law regarding punishment and suspension of students. That law is called SB 419 which prohibits schools, including Charter schools, from suspending students for willful defiance.

"SB 419 is designed to keep kids in school by eliminating willful defiance suspension in grades 4-5 and banning them in grades 6-8 for five years". The Bill was signed into law by the Governor, Gavin Newsom in September 2019, effective July 1, 2020. The author of the bill explains:

"SB 419 puts the needs of kids first," Senator Nancy Skinner said. "Ending willful defiance suspensions will keep kids in school where they belong and where teachers and counselors can help them thrive." Really? Are you talking about the same teachers and counselors your Bill is encouraging students to defy their authority?

That means that Senator Skinner thinks she can make students "thrive" without discipline. She is expecting the teachers and counselors to make the students "thrive" in the midst of student "willful defiance" of authority. Good luck! The bill passed the Senate with a 31-8 vote while it passed the House of Assembly with a 58 to 17 vote. The bill cited some of the willful defiance to include "a student not removing a hat or hoodie in class." Once again, our liberal politicians in California exhibit their "wisdom and expertise" once more. A student willfully disrespects staff by refusing to remove his or her hat or hoodie in class when asked to do so by the staff and there is no punishment! That sends a terrible message. Instead, the Bill wants the student to engage in a so-called restorative justice "conflict resolution" with the teacher or staff member. What a way to go! Do they realize the multiple effects of a student's willful defiance of authority that is left unpunished? That could become the beginning of all kinds of societal ills of crimes, drugs, insubordination, not complying with police orders and incarceration in the making. That opens in a student's mind that there is no discipline for unlawful actions. That same message is consciously or unconsciously passed on to other students in other States and beyond. No wonder these Politicians and Administrators send their own children to private and religious schools where discipline produces well rounded students.

This Senate Bill was introduced and authored by Senator Nancy Skinner, a California Democrat from Berkeley, California 9th Senatorial district. Do you know what her issue with the old law was? She told us "That State data shows students of color are more likely to be suspended for willful defiance than white students." Did she really mean to say that? "Yes", she did. This is exactly what is the problem with our politics and nation of late. It is all about "black votes". So, Senator Skinner and her liberal colleagues are saying that if students of color are willfully misbehaving and disrespecting authority, the appropriate solution is to abolish discipline in the whole system for five years instead of punishing the culprits' insubordination and restore order in the school. Why do these politicians see everything as a race and color issue? This is the politics of divide and conquer for votes. It is no longer about the offense and school discipline but the color and race of the offender. For the politicians it is better to win minority votes than maintaining discipline in the school system. The irony is that it is these same politicians who are responsible for the indiscipline exhibited by the colored students in the first place. It comes down to lack of concern on the part of these policy makers, who have enough money to send their own children to private schools. They send their children to disciplined and private schools where there is a dress code: no hats, no hoodies in the classroom, no oversize or baggy clothes where a student could hide guns etc. They know the right thing to do; but they don't want to be realistic to the facts. Instead of doing the right thing to uplift the colored students, who are lagging behind in school, they want to play the politics of appeasement by removing discipline from the school system in the State of liberal California. While they claim to fight for the colored students, they really don't care about them; they only put them down and set them up for failure and at the same time get the students' parents to vote for them. If they had a stubborn child in their own house, would they abolish all house rules?

Children in poor neighborhoods need a well ordered, well-disciplined special curriculum to succeed in their academic pursuit. The

133

Republicans floated the idea of Charter Schools to make sure that minority students, who are trapped in public schools, are rescued. Unfortunately, the Democrats don't want Charter Schools to see the light of day because that would alienate them with the Teachers' Union. Moreover, Charter schools would liberate the black people they have held hostage for over fifty years. The reality that Senator Skinner, her fellow Democrats in the California Senate and State Assembly with the State Governor did not want to deal with is the conflict between the powerful Teachers' Union that funds their elections and the competition presented by Charter Schools, which not only teach discipline, but have lifted up minority students to academic excellence. Charter schools are tailored to the student's need, not the 'one size fits all' model of many public schools in a system that has students whose parents have disparity in incomes and neighborhoods. What these disadvantaged students need is a "disciplined, tailored students' need" curriculum. If the lawmakers wanted to lift up these minority students, they would be making available more Charter schools to take care of these failing minority schools. But they don't. That would release the hostages, and the Democrats would no longer take their votes for granted. One would ask: why do the Teachers' Union not want the existence of more Charter schools? They don't want competition with Charter schools. This kind of competition would make the public schools; the teachers and school administrators wake up and do the right thing for minority students. But they won't want that. If Charter schools lift disadvantaged students with less dollars, the American people would be asking why huge amounts of taxpayer dollars are spent in public schools while there are still poor students' indiscipline and poor educational performance and chaotic streets. They don't want that revelation and comparison with Charter schools. Since the teachers' union and school administrators don't want Charter schools to increase, the politicians they sponsor in elections don't want Charter schools to increase either because of the Teachers' Union's money. Consequently, poor parents are left out in the cold. So, who is for California colored children and America's colored children? That is the big elephant in the room that nobody wants to address.

It has been known for a long time that public school employees have become political operatives because they are in bed with politicians. But since this marriage between the Union and the political class is the 'big elephant' in the room because of its political cloud, some parents opted to send their children to private schools, where there is discipline and real education going on. The measure of discipline in private schools does not give room for a student to bring drugs and weapons into the school. Apart from the seriousness and high level of educational standard in private schools, there are 'dress codes', discipline, moral education and 'God' in school. That is why parents are willing to sacrifice and pay, not only their portion of state and federal taxes that fund public schools, but they are also willing to additionally pay high school fees to train their children in private and religious schools. Unfortunately, not all-American parents can afford to pay to send their children to private schools. That was why some politicians of goodwill started to float the idea of school vouchers for poor parents to take their children or wards to any school of their choice, where they see more value. For the same reasons already stated, some politicians have done all in their power to stifle school vouchers and Charter Schools. Even though the public-school administrators have something to do with how Charter schools work and operate, Charter schools have their independence in the discipline and method they apply in teaching these poor minority students, who are coming from a different environment. This is all spelled out in the "charter" or agreement between the traditional public-school authorities and the new system (charter schools). Though minority communities do not normally vote for Republicans, yet the Republicans have been in the forefront of finding alternatives to traditional public schools, to help poor and minority students to minimize poverty and crimes in those neighborhoods. There have been politicians who have proposed having more Charter schools in several States in the Federation. But several Democrat States have not been in favor of such proposals because of their relationship with the powerful Teachers' Union which is opposed to Charter Schools. More Charter Schools would reduce the number of Public Schools and consequently teachers. Initially in States like California, Connecticut, Illinois, Michigan, New Mexico etc, Democratic gubernatorial candidates openly campaigned against charter schools. Later, under President Obama, some Democrats saw it fit to give it a try for whatever reason.

That is why at the point of the Charter schools' debate, it seemed to have been a bipartisan venture when President Obama and the Democrats came on board to join Republicans to establish more Charter Schools. So, what happened later? It appears that the Democrats joined the experiment to prove the Charter school concept wrong. But now that Charter school is in motion and doing well, it seems that everybody is not happy about its success. This is why so many people don't like politics the way some people play it. Success is played down because of political party differences? A New York Political Columnist, Jonathan Chait wrote about the success of Charter Schools:

"Charter Schools have produced dramatic learning gains for low-income minority students. In city after city, from New York to New Orleans, Charters have found ways to reach the children, who have been most consistently failed by traditional schools. And yet the second outcome of the Charter-school breakthrough has been a bitter backlash within the Democratic party", he said. He went further to say that "the political standing of the idea has moved in the opposite direction of the data, as two powerful forces - unions and progressive activists - have come to regard charter schools as a plutonic assault on public education and an ideological betrayal." Auch!

Mr. Jonathan Chait also quoted the leader of the Democrats, President Biden talking to a crowd of voters in South Carolina during the 2019 Democratic primary:

"I am not a charter-school fan because it takes away the options available and the money for public schools", then Vice President Biden said.

Really? That utterance from a Presidential candidate came loud and clear that he was not about how to help minority students. The Presidential candidate was not interested in how to better the poor minority children to score better in school nationally and internationally as well as becoming the best citizens they can be. Instead, his interest was to maintain the relationship between his party and the powerful Teachers' Union. Yet more than 80% of the parents of these minority students voted for Mr. Biden simply because he is a Democrat. That means that bringing up minority students to standard is not a priority for Mr. Biden and the Democrats. What is important is taking care of the donors - the teachers' union, which in turn will make available the money to win elections and reelections. When he became the President, Jonathan investigated what was the inside debate about who would be President Biden's Education Secretary. This is what Jonathan found out:

"To head the Department of Education, Biden floated the names of fierce critics of Charter schools including the ex-president of the country's largest teacher union and former dean of Howard University School of education, who called urban charters "schemes" that are really all about controlling urban land."

Just "schemes"? Really? That confirms all that Biden said about how he felt about charter schools and where he is taking education in the nation.

On November 14, 2023, Jacob Fischler and Cole Claybourn had this to say about Charter schools:

"The rise of charter schools changed the education marketplace and provided new options, even for parents without the means or desire to send their students to private school." Quoting Mr. Bacon they continued:

"Chaters added more options and different models of schools to the system which usually gives parents more choices." says James Bacon, former staffing director at Boston Public schools and current director of outreach and operations at education technology firm, Edficiency, wrote in an email. Still quoting him, they went on to say:

"In many ways, the biggest pros and cons of charter schools stem from the same fact: That in most cases, charter schools are given more freedom than traditional public schools. Given the ability to operate through those agreements, charter schools can tailor their curriculum, academic focus, staffing ratios, discipline policies and other matters generally decided at the school district or state board level. In exchange for that flexibility charter schools are supposed to be accountable to parents and state and local governments that authorize them."

This is the kind of educational diversity and choice needed to lift children in poor and low-income neighborhoods of America to minimize crime and deterioration of those neighborhoods. The question is: will the adults in the room let it succeed and continue? So far, the adults in the room have been part of the problem and the so-called leaders of these neighborhoods have been involved in the corruption and betrayal of the students in low-income neighborhoods. Those neighborhoods continue to vote every two or four years for the same people who despise Charter schools for their neighborhoods. Why? The individual leaders in the poor neighborhoods are paid off by the politicians. In return the paid local leaders mislead and confuse the parents to bring out the votes.

The solution to youth and gang crimes in American cities are in plain view. The lack of implementation of the solution is deliberate and political. Frank Adamson, an associate professor of education policy and leadership studies at California State University - Sacramento, who studied Charter schools' performance, said:

"The flexibility that Charter schools are afforded in our system means that they try different things with varying results. Some schools may focus on arts or theater. Others may emphasize science, technology, engineering and mathematics or STEM", (Science, Technology, Engineering Mathematics).

Fischler and Claybourn think that Charter schools were growing at the beginning in the 1980s and 1990s. Charter schools were operating schools in about 35 States of the federation in the 2000 - 2001 school year. It rose to 45 States, according to the Education Commission of the States. Charter schools had about 3.7 million students during the 2011-2012 school year or about 7% of all public schools, according to North Carolina Employment Security Commission (NCESC). That's up from 2 million students enrolled in Charter schools in the 2011-2012 school year, about 4% of public-school students. Reacting to that, the director of the center on Reinventing Public Education, a research organization inside Arizona State University's Mary Lou Fulton Teacher College, Ms. Robin Lake said:

"There were a lot of investments made by the Federal government through startup funds and foundations in high-quality charter school models and expansion replication of those models. There was a lot of enthusiasm about making those opportunities more accessible to more kids, and there was demand as well. I think those two dynamics came together and we saw pretty explosive growth. The studies that have been done about Charter schools in urban areas show pretty unequivocally that they have been doing their job in terms of narrowing the achievement gap. I would not say closing it, because that's a tall order, but we should still aim high", she said.

That assessment seems to be a realistic way to look at Charter schools. Ms. Lake objectively sees what is working to raise the standard of education in minority and poor neighborhoods in America and is asking that the government should continue the advancement of Charter schools and funding them adequately. She is not a politician. She saw the enthusiasm of making what is working for minority children "more accessible for more kids". Moreover, she noted: "the studies that have been done about charter schools in urban areas show pretty unequivocally that they have been doing their job in terms of narrowing the achievement gap". Isn't that what any fair-minded American, and in fact, all Americans want for poor American children left behind academically by the public school system? Is this not what our politicians should want for children in their constituency, knowing that if these low-income and poor children continue to be left behind, they would become our new school-dropouts, our neighborhood gang members, our new drug addicts, prisoners and homeless people sooner or later? On what side are these politicians? Senator Skinner and her Democrat colleagues in California want these minority students only to feel good by not learning academic discipline in school. That is their solution to minority students' insubordination. One does not need to be a politician to know what works if one is honest and sincere. That calls into serious question the honesty and sincerity of a lot of our politicians. Mr. Jonathan Chait has told us that "in city after city, from New York to New Orleans, Charter schools have produced dramatic learning gains for low-income minority students". Why then do Democrats and Teachers' Union, supposed adults in the room, not want to continue to create more of what is helping to raise the academic standard of students in poor neighborhoods, which they claim to be fighting for? Why do they not want to eliminate poverty, and crimes in those neighborhoods? Perhaps getting these neighborhoods out of poverty would affect how they vote in elections. Someone is not telling the American people the truth here. The reality is that the education of minority students is the best way to cut down on poverty, crimes and homelessness in America. The irony is that the leaders of these minority groups betray the people and help to elect and reelect the same people who are part of the problem.

Some Democrats, like President Biden, are saying that Charter schools are taking the "money" for public schools. Is it not a shame that a president would exclude poor students from low-income neighborhoods from money allocated for the education of all American children? For these children to go to non-public schools, since public schools have failed to cater for the needs of these students, their parents would have to be able to pay their tuition and fees in private or mission schools. But we know that the parents of these students are poor and cannot pay their regular tax and still pay for private schools. Yet some politicians are saying that public funds should not be used to educate these children in a structured school that will prevent raising more criminals and lawless youths. They see taxpayer money put into Charter schools as money taken from public schools as if students in Charter schools are not our children and the children of taxpayers also. It is appalling to hear President Biden say that he is not a fan of charter schools which "have found ways to reach the children who have been mostly consistently failed by traditional schools", according to Mr. Jonathan Chait, a New York political columnist.

The President is not alone in this view. Almost all Democrats express the same sentiment. Look at what Ms. Diane Ravitch, a Democrat and a historian of education, an educational policy analyst, a research professor at New York University's Steinhardt School of Culture, Education and Human Development, said about Charter schools in 2019:

Quoting Ms. Diane Ravitch, Jacob Fischer and Cole Claybourn said: "The election of Trump and the appointment of Betsy De Vos clarified that school choice is a right-wing issue pushed by the Waltons, the De Vos family, the Koch brothers and every red state governor", March 18,.2019.

This utterance by Ms. Diane Ravitch is more direct and to a certain extent more sincere as to what their objection to Charter schools is all about. Politics and hatred of Mr. Trump seems to be the only point here. How does this type of hatred help the poor students that Charter schools are helping in real time? What does having a school or system designed to help poor students in low-income neighborhoods to catch up with their counterparts in rich neighborhoods have to do with "right wing issues pushed by the Waltons, … and every red state governor"? Her comment is all about politics and hatred of Mr. Trump and the Republican party. It is not about Charter Schools and how to help underprivileged students to benefit from the Charter schools; it is rather about Trump and the people who are trying to help the poor students to "narrow the achievement gap", created by the public schools which have over the years failed the underprivileged students in poor neighborhoods. One would think that the focus should be on the achievement of our students irrespective of who made it happen, political friend or foe. How did America come to this type of political hatred that people are willing to throw underprivileged American students under the bus to score cheap political points? Ms Diane Ravitch was willing to put her education and place in society on the line to put a wedge on a good program introduced by someone from another political party at the expense of our children. That is way too below the belt. Her whole being has been against Charter Schools for selfish reasons. Look at some of her writings and titles:

"The Myth of Charter Schools". "Dark History of School Choice" and "The Death and life of the Great American School System: How testing and Choice are undermining Education. This is perhaps one other reason why many Americans are fed up with politics and why America is the way it is today in terms of crimes and homelessness.

Let us see how researchers look at education in our country today. Remember that the purpose of research is to find out what is working and what is not working in any system or organization to improve the system or organization. Some people have devoted time, money and energy to investigate our educational system vis a vis public and private/charter schools. Emily Pierce, a freelance writer, who previously spent 17 years covering Congress and White House for Roll Call and Cole Claybourn, a reporter for U.S News on August 29, 2023 regarding parents choosing schools for their children quote Myra Mc Govern, a spokesperson for National Association of Independent Schools as saying that it all comes down to what is best for each child. "Individual needs of the child should shape the choice for parents", Myra said. They went on to say that: "Research has consistently shown that private schools tend to perform better on standardized tests. The National Assessment of Educational Progress (NAEP), which is often referred to as "the nation's report card" assesses both public and private schools' students in subjects such as mathematics, reading, science and writing. The most recent NAEP data shows what other research has found. Private school students score better in almost all subjects. For example, eighth grade private school students averaged about 20 points higher than public school or charter students on the NAEP reading test in 2022. Fourth grade private school students had nearly the same advantage in average scores."

"On college entry tests such as the SAT, National Association of Independent Schools (NAIS), found that students in private schools consistently outperformed their public-school peers in all subject areas. While private schools appear on paper to promise better educational outcomes for their students, some scholars have attempted to dig deeper than just test scores to find out if private schools actually increase student success".

They pointed to Dr. Robert C. Pianta, who led a study published in 2018 that examined academic, social, psychological and attained outcomes, says he found student success is more directly related to family attributes, such as having college educated parents and higher incomes, than which school they attend. He said: "When you compare children who went to private school (for an average of six years) with those who only went to public school, any apparent benefits of private schooling - higher test scores, for example - are entirely attributable to parents' education and income" he says. "The fact that they went to private school does not account for any difference we might see". But that is the point of Charter Schools. We know that the parents of students in Charter Schools are neither college graduates nor rich.

Christopher Lubinski, a professor at Indiana University and coauthor of the book, "The Public School and Advantage: Why Public Schools Outperform Private Schools", agrees saying, "whether it's a public school or private school is not necessarily the defining factor. Private schools tend to score better on tests... But we found that family background differences more than explain the difference between Public and Private school test scores".

The journalists went on to ask: "How do students from low-income families perform"?

Megan Austin, a principal researcher at the American Institutes for Research, looked at the success of students who participated in Indiana's public funded private school voucher program, which is aimed at students from low-income socioeconomic backgrounds and skews heavily toward the parochial schools that participate in voucher programs. She says that students using vouchers to attend private schools were somewhat less successful than those who were attending without voucher, but that "both types of students ... were less likely than traditional public-school students to ever fail a course, or to ever be suspended in high school, and they were more likely to enroll in college within one year of High School graduation".

That Is good news for voucher and charter schools. Isn't that what every American should want for low-income students to lift them up from poverty? If America can have students from low-income families who are in charter or voucher schools and they are "less likely to fail a course, or to ever be suspended in high school, and ... were more likely to enroll in college within one year of High school graduation" than traditional public-school students, we would drastically cut down on juvenile crimes in the nation. That would be the goal of real and practical education where students acquire the knowledge and discipline of law-abiding citizens of America instead of the current lawlessness that we have experienced among our youths in public schools today. Unfortunately, this noble goal cannot be achieved without the help of our political class in Federal and State establishments. And some politicians are not playing.

Judging from what Senator Skinner of California State Senate proposed for California schools in her bill (SB 419) above, there is no way to achieve the goal of education for low-income students of America, who are already handicapped in a lot of ways. Some of them act out in school because of the poor upbringing at home. They act out because they have no structure at home and in some cases, there are no fathers in the house. Instead of helping them by giving them structure and discipline, Skinner and her group disappointed them with the ridiculous SB 419. To rescue them, these students need a structured school like Charter to get the knowledge and discipline, which Ms. Nancy Skinner and her fellow Democrats are robbing them of through her legislation - SB 419. This legislation which claims to be for the good of students of color is making already willful defiant students more defiant and likely drop-outs. If, according to SB 419, "data shows that students of color are more likely to be suspended for willful defiance than white students", one would think that the solution would be to go for a structured system like Charter schools to bring such students to compliance. Instead, the sponsors of the Bill preferred to water-down discipline for both the white and the colored students. In fact, Bill SB 419 is not only telling the students of color to continue to be defiant, but it also invites the other students to do the same since there is no consequence for willful defiance.

Talking about colored students, Ms. Skinner seemed to have deliberately forgotten other data regarding races and colors in sports and other areas. Did she forget that there are an overwhelming and unproportional number of blacks playing Basketball in the NBA than whites? These black players make millions of dollars a year and that is a good thing to lift their families and perhaps, their neighborhoods. It is called talent, hard work, discipline and dedication in those sports. It is the same discipline Senator Skinner and her fellow Democrats in California removed from the school's system through SB 419 that fashioned the success of these colored athletes in NBA and other sports. To succeed in any endeavor, one needs discipline not overindulgence for political advantage. Not everybody is gifted the same way. These black players receive rewards for a job well done, not because of their color but because of their industry exhibited in sacrifice and discipline during their training. The reverse is also true; bad behavior merits punishment. If most black students are unruly in the school system, they should be disciplined accordingly, not because of their color but because of their actions. That will help mold their character for future use.

It is curious that Senator Skinner has not proposed any law to require a quota system in the National Basketball Association (NBA) simply because there are more blacks in the NBA than whites. Is Senator Nancy Skinner not aware that there are more blacks, per capita, incarcerated in prison in the United States of America, whereas the black population in America is by far smaller than the white population? Why has she not proposed a law to impose a quota system on the number of incarcerations in California to level the incarceration 'playing field'? It is this kind of law proposed by Senator Skinner and her fellows that is the cause of more blacks incarcerated in our prison system today by throwing them "soft balls" and expecting them to excel; teaching them indiscipline (willful defiance) in school and at the same time expecting them to be disciplined and crime-free in the real world. What a manifestation of stupidity to be reelected into the State Senate! It has always been about politics for a lot of these politicians, and it is a pity. If it does not benefit the politician, it is a non-issue. It is not about the good and future of the black or minority students or the people. It is about the benefit to the politicians involved. Elections and reelections are the key to what some politicians are interested in and they will do it even to disadvantage the children in school. They can afford to send their children to private schools, anyway. Youth delinquency in America is caused by adults.

In Virginia, the State legislature passed a law requiring parental notification before any minor goes for any gender surgery from school. Some school board members (politicians) have threatened to disobey the law because they are backed by the political power hitters in Washington DC. The same thing is happening in states like California, New Jersey, Connecticut, Colorado to name a few. Note that all these States are run by the same Party. It is rather unfortunate that parents, who send their children to school, have no say about the health of their children anymore. In Biden's America, children belong to the government and not the parents. Politics! What an insult! All this is to appease the LGBTQIA+ community, which has no children of their own to begin with. What do they care about the welfare of these children, one would ask? They want men to marry men and women marry women, knowing that there is no chance for the so-called marriages producing children. All Americans should be asking: What is their interest in children? Just meditate on that question for a while. What is their interest in children when they have "no horse in the race"? Does anybody have a better answer than that they want to recruit other people's children into their community? Is that fair game? This is insanity run amok and nobody is asking: who really owns these children? Do they have parents? Who takes care of these children when they are sick? Who feeds and clothes these children? Who is responsible for the overall welfare of these children - the parents or the school or state? Yet politicians let transgender community decide how to educate children. Think about that. Some Politician's silence in this matter is one other way politicians corrupt the young.

Just recently the Catholic Archdiocese of Denver, Colorado sued the State of Colorado Department of Early Childhood and Universal Preschool program for passing a law requiring that any participating school (like the Catholic schools) must "accept any applicant without regard to a student or family's religion, sexual orientation, or gender identity". According to the diocese, such a law violates the First Amendment right of individuals and institution's right of maintaining their Catholic identity and teaching. That is why the Catholic schools are established in the first place. The leftist politicians of the State of Colorado have no right to force the Catholic Church to go against their moral teaching to accommodate the LGBTQIA+ community. The money used to run the Early Childhood and Universal Preschool program belongs to the people, the parents, grandparents and relatives of these students, not the politicians. The government has no money. It does not make sense for the government to deny parents and taxpayers the opportunity of participating in such programs operated with taxpayer funds because they refuse to give up their first amendment religious right and freedom. That is what happens when LGBTQIA+ sympathizers are running the school system. This is another way politicians are corrupting the young people of America.

But the Supreme Court has ruled it unconstitutional to force or coerce a person or group to accept another person's or group's beliefs or ideology in place of one's own belief. In the "Masterpiece Cakeshop Ltd v Colorado Civil Rights Commission'', the Supreme Court ruled in favor of Masterpiece Cakeshop Ltd. In a 7-2 decision, the U. S. Supreme Court ruled that it is unconstitutional to ask Jack Phillips, owner of Masterpiece Cakeshop Ltd to design and bake a special wedding cake for Charlie Craig and David Mullins's same sex marriage, which he, Phillips, considers against his religious belief. The First Amendment rights enshrined in the Constitution since its inception comes before gay marriage rights of yesterday.

Politicians are at it again to lower the standard of education, which could increase the number of school dropouts and future criminals in the country. It is always the politicians who cause the problems that affect teens and society eventually. Youth delinquency caused by adults in power is a shame. The school boards in Portland Oregon, New York, California and others are making waves again. These Democrat politicians do not care about the academic growth of the students or the eradication of crimes in the nation. They will play politics with everything including the wellbeing and progress of American children. According to "The Washington Free Beacon", in Portland, Oregon public school is workshopping new "equitable grading practices" that bar teachers from assigning "zeros" to students who cheat or fail to turn in assignments. Take a minute to digest that. Teachers are barred by politicians from assigning a zero to a student who does not turn in his or her assignment to the teacher. What grade does a teacher assign a student who did not do any academic work? Where is the reasoning? It goes back to no consequences for bad behavior. In other words, the teacher is advised to give marks to students who do not merit any marks to be "politically correct". These Democrat politicians in the State of Oregon, through legislation, are telling teachers to turn students out without any learning or training. If these children don't learn or graduate properly, they become a nuisance and liability to society despite the high salaries paid to these administrators by the taxpayers. It is fine with them that their actions are purposely preparing the students for failure and join the culture of crimes. How did we get here? Where did they get these men and women?

You may want to know the reason for this "wise" Oregon new approach. The board, of course, told us. They said that the district's initiative aims at addressing "racial disparities" and "inequities" in grading. There you go again. And we pay these board members? These people see nothing but race issues which only divide America just to score political points among minority voters. This is a shame on people earning big salaries paid by the people and parents and grandparents and relatives of the students entrusted to their care to educate. But they have nothing to show for the salaries they receive, thanks to the adults and policy makers in Portland, Oregon. Their interest is not to encourage scholarship in the students to study hard to be better in life and benefit themselves and society. Their interest is focused on "racial disparities" and "inequities" in grading. The correct question and concern of these legislatures should have been to find out if the grading of individuals is what the individuals deserve. The way these administrators know to promote equity is to pass out students who were not educated. Promote every student to the next class for "equity" sake (DEI) and make underperforming students happy instead of encouraging and helping challenged students to work hard to succeed. Is pushing out unschooled and uneducated children to society thereby turning them out into the world of crime, the best these Oregon school administrators can do for their constituencies? The unfortunate children cut up in this situation must somehow survive in society like everybody else. With the hands they have been dealt with by the policy makers, the only option left for them is to make a living out of crime. Unscrupulous politicians are the problems. Their policies make criminals out of young people. The aim of these politicians is to tell underperforming students that they cannot make it and at the same time they don't want to make them feel bad about it. As for the students who are doing better, these board members pull them down, so they don't make the other students feel bad. They make every student intellectually blind to avoid making some people feel bad. "Feeling"? Feelings don't educate children. Is that why parents send their children to school? Do parents send their children to school to be pitied, or do they send them to school to be educated?

The Portland district's policy makers also call for no penalties for student late work and no grading for both homework and "non-academic factors" like class "participation, attendance, effort, attitude and behavior". This is incredible. They don't want discipline. They don't want to produce responsible students and citizens for the nation, and they wonder why such states and cities have high school dropouts, high crime rates, high drug addiction, high suicides and homelessness. This calls into question the reason why parents send their children to public schools like these. If homework, class attendance, attitude of the student, the effort of the student, class participation of the student and behavior of the student are ignored, what will the teacher use to evaluate the students' performance? Oh, I forgot. There is no evaluation or grading. Every student is pushed to the next level for "equity's sake". This is exactly the reason American students cannot compete with students from Asia and Europe and Africa. American students are now ranked behind twenty-five countries in grade level Reading, Science and Mathematics. Is this still the United States of America, the Superpower? Where do they get these board members who are desperately pulling America down? The only thing the children need is an opportunity to succeed. It is the politician's way of getting the vote of minorities whose children are under-performing. So, when there is no grading or when everybody in class gets the same grade, the parents of minority students are deceived to think that their children are doing just fine in school. Parents and any well-meaning Americans should be disturbed and outraged by these trending measures aimed at our children by career politicians without conscience. Are these people friends or foes, one may ask? Look at the facts and the trends. To this Portland proposal slated to start in 2025, the outreach director at Parental rights group, Parents Defending Education, Erika Sanzi, said that Portland's "equitable grading practices" hurt both struggling and high-achieving students. Exactly the point! There are no winners. So, what is their goal when they know, I suppose, that they are setting the two groups of students up to fail? Their goal is nothing but their political success. It is for the same reason these politicians and school administrators don't want Charter or Home schools or School Vouchers to succeed, lest parents see public schools as they are in fact through competition. Their deception is the reason we have so many failing schools, so many depressed school drop-outs, so many young drug addicts and homeless dwellers. It is for these same reasons that young people don't see any reason to live and so many commit suicide, so many of them have raised crimes to a new profession. These politicians should all be voted out.

The question now is: What do these communities benefit from these stupid laws and policies? No communities benefit from these self-serving policies. The high achieving students from middle class neighborhoods lose out and downgrade their academic achievements while the low-income neighborhoods of minority groups of blacks and Hispanics get worse and perhaps drop out of school and get on the fast lane of life. These latter groups were the reason the politicians made these policies; the parents of these minority students control a big chunk of the political votes the Democrats need to win in any given election. For years and years, the minority groups have been the bargaining chips for Democrats in any election, local, state and national. Every two and four years the same scenarios play out. But nobody stops to ask: what are the benefits of these policies to minority communities? Nobody is asking: why are youth crimes, drug epidemics, gang violence, homicides of black on black ("The Crips and Bloods" in some areas) and Hispanic on Hispanic (The "Norteños and Surenos" in some areas) crimes and homelessness, more prevalent in those same cities and states run by Democrat Governors and Mayors and politicians who make these policies? Have they, by these reckless policies, removed the "racial disparities" and "inequities" between whites and blacks and other minorities for more than sixty years? Every two or four years, the same people come to whip up "equity" and "racial" sentiments and make promises to eradicate them just to get the votes. When they get into office, they quietly say in their mind to the people: "see you again in two or four or six years"! Unfortunately, the ordinary people are deceived by their local leaders; they do it repeatedly. Why? The leaders in these minority neighborhoods are heavily rewarded financially by the candidates seeking elective offices for their support. These minority neighborhood leaders sell their neighborhoods for money. The people morally and physically go through this political vicious circle, which plays every election year.

It is the same madness in the same Democrat states and cities. Recently the California District Attorney was suing one of the school districts in California. According to a CNN report, California's Attorney General sues Chino Valley Unified School district over policy requiring parental notification when students change gender identification. According to CNN reporters, Alisha Ebrahimi and Andy Rose, "the lawsuit filed on August 28, 2023, challenges the policy in a 4-1 vote by the district in July 2023. District Attorney Rob Bonta argues that the policy violates the State Constitution's guarantee of a right to privacy and to receive a public education without discrimination." The lawsuit states: "The District has no compelling interest in singling out transgender and gender non-affirming students to different and unfavorable treatment." It continues to say that "these students are currently under the threat of being outed to their parents against their will, and many fear that the district's policy will force them to make a choice: either to "walk back" their constitutional and statutorily protected rights to gender identity and gender expression, or face the risk of emotional, physical harm from non-affirming or unaccepting parents or guardian."

This is ridiculous. Isn't it unfortunate how these lawyers always drag in "privacy" into their ridiculous argument. We are talking about children as young as 12 years. Since when did America give 12-year-olds the power to withhold things as serious as sex change from their parents? This is exactly what Chino Unified District is trying to do under this law by protecting parental rights. Unfortunately, according to Los Angeles reporters, Priscella Vega and Hannah Wiley, a San Bernardino Superior Court Judge, Thomas Garza, granted the state's request for a temporary restraining order. That means that the court has ordered the Chino Valley Unified School District to hold off on enforcing the new policy until further notice. There you go again with judges playing politics with children's lives in a situation where even brute animals in the bush know that children belong to their parents, who brought them into the world and take care of them more than anyone else can. The president of the Chino Valley Unified district, Sonja Shaw, reacting to the lawsuit said:

"The lawsuit was not a surprise as State officials had repeatedly taken steps to shut parents out of their children's lives."

District Attorney Rob Bonta knows that Washington, FBI, DOJ, and all the other Federal machinery got his back on the subject. He is there to take orders from above. I am almost sure he would not like to send his children to the kind of school he is advocating for. "His Master's voice" must be heeded to. Deep inside the DA knows that the California "privacy" law he cited does not trump parental rights. But the Superior Court Judge gave him what he knew was coming. That is how the game is played here on children by adults. It is once more politicians who mislead young people in America.

Fortunately, some parents are fighting back. In a case in liberal California, an NBC News reporter Julianne McShane wrote:

"A California School District has paid $100,000 to settle a lawsuit over administrator's alleged support for a student's gender transition, which purportedly unfolded without the knowledge of the child's mother, according to court documents. The Spreckels Union School District, about 60 miles south of San Jose, agreed to the payout in June, about a year after the mother, Jessica Konen, filed the lawsuit. The lawsuit alleged that the district and three of its employees "secretly convinced" Konen's child that the minor was bisexual and transgender and encouraged the student to conceal it from Konen, allegedly violating her 14th Amendment rights to direct her child's upbringing." McShane continued: "In a statement to NBC News, one of Konen's lawyers, Harmeet Dhillon, a Republican party official and the founder of the center for American Liberty, a conservative legal nonprofit group said: "Konen's triumph strongly underscores the principle that parents, not schools, have a natural right to shape their child's upbringing". The lawyer continues: "This settlement sends a loud message to all school districts; attempting to secretly transition a child without parental notification or consent will lead to substantial repercussions," Dhillon said. "Natural Right" are the operative words in the lawyer's statement. It is rather unfortunate that the Biden administration has ceded that right to the LGBTQIA+'s-controlled schools.

Parents and some school boards are fighting back to assert the rights of parents concerning their children. "In Texas, a school board in a suburb 30 miles outside of Houston approved a new policy on Monday that requires parents to be told if their students choose to identify as transgender or nonbinary, or if they want to change their name or use different pronouns at school." That is how a few Districts and parents are trying to assume their rightful positions in society. But the hostile, current wind is against them 9 times out of 10. The stinking odor in a skunk is not on the skin, but inside the bone. These politicians cannot help themselves; their problems are deep rooted. Yet their bad actions affect our children adversely.

CHAPTER THIRTEEN: TEENAGERS, CRIMES, DRUG-USE

CRIMES:

Thomas Hine, writing for The American Heritage History Magazine, September 1999 edition, volume 50, issue 5, page 1 started an article on "Teenagers and Crime", like this:

"They are armed. They are dangerous. They are our children."

That says it all and the picture was bleak then. If this was true in nineteen ninety-nine, it is twice true today. This is a reality we would wish was not true. But unfortunately, it is true, and we are losing our children and the government and some politicians seem to be part of the problem and are waiting for the other shoe to drop. In human development, teenage years are awkward and difficult. It is also an impressionable period in a teen's development. Their mind and reasoning abilities are very naive and pliable, ready to absorb and harness the good advice of adults in their lives for better development in the years ahead or unfortunately bad advice and cues from adults in their lives and end up on the wrong side of the law. This is the most unfortunate part of it; that adults in their lives can and do mislead them in a lot of ways. That betrayal is what has left America in the situation it is today - a state of violence, crimes, immorality and Godlessness. What a tragedy!

At this teenage stage young people crave for knowledge and all kinds of things in between. They are like sponges which will absorb anything that comes their way, the good, the bad and the ugly. This is the time they need good direction and advice the most in their lives. Influencers, religious leaders, political operators and parents have the best opportunities to fashion the next generation during this period, if they would seize the day. Unfortunately, it is at this stage that some politicians, government and courts deprive them of the opportunity to know God first and foremost in school. But when adults do not show up, teens make up things for themselves as they go because it is in their nature to want to do something. That is the nature of teenagers all over the world. Teens at this stage like clear and definite instructions. Every young person looks up to adults, including parents and government to show them the way to follow. But when this desired guidance is ignored, denied or skewed or unhealthy when given, it puts teens in a head spin that most likely lands them in a countercultural ground which later develops into other more serious problems for themselves and society at large. Ambiguity is not the way to deal with teens.

When teens are disappointed by adults, it demoralizes and makes them act up and become anti-social. They shut down the window of communication. It should be remembered that these children are only thirteen up to nineteen years old operating in a society more complex than their brain could absorb. Teen antisocial behavior is manifested in smoking, stealing, doing drugs, experimenting on sex, cutting school and eventually dropping out of school for some. When a teenager drops out of school, he or she could become a time bomb if there is no immediate adult intervention.

Generally, education is an individual's "meal ticket" for life. Without this meal ticket an individual teen can become anything negative under the sun waiting to be rescued in some cases if there is a helping hand. The sky's the limit of the havoc he or she can cause to self and or society. There is a potential for specializing in one or more of the crimes he or she has been toying with. A once nice, normal, altar boy teenager suddenly becomes a monster, drug addict, alcoholic, thief, gangbanger and a societal misfit. With a combination of some of the bad habits in a teen's repertoire, a girl is very likely to become pregnant as a teenager and subsequently a mother or a habitual abortionist or street girl; if a boy he is likely to become a teenage father, a sex offender or a prisoner. Ordinarily this is not their vision for life. The government, the adults in their life or both have dropped the ball on them.

As a school drop-out, a teenager is not likely to have a good job to take care of himself, a spouse and perhaps children. To make ends meet, such a teen will by necessity hang around bad characters and very likely engage in all kinds of crimes to keep body and soul together and maintain all the acquired addictions of alcohol and or drugs. Why? He did not collect his "meal tick" in school. In this state of mind, the teens become anti progress. Other people's legitimate success becomes offensive and irritates them. When they become bitter because they don't have what others have, they feel entitled to anything out there and they are willing to use force to get them. The rich and accomplished people in society automatically become enemies just because they are well off. They blame everybody else but themselves for their poverty. Stealing, looting, prostitution, rape, all become legitimate ways to survive. It will not take long before he or she ends up in prison because of one or more of the bad habits and or addictions. By its nature and the way politicians designed them, prisons have a way of liberating or further enslaving their residents. Out of a hundred teenage inmates incarcerated, about seventy will become habitual and hardened criminals, in and out of prisons for a greater part of their lives. This is the tragedy when teens and adults in their lives make that initial mistake of neglecting teens or teens dropping out of school without collecting their "meal ticket". On the part of the government and adults neglecting their duty toward teens, this is what you get. And on the part of teens carelessly dropping out of school without an alternative solid plan of trade or survival skills or profession, a life of crime or lawlessness becomes their new reality. Any way you look at it, they become losers, and the society suffers what we see on our streets and neighborhoods today. For those who play politics with people's lives, especially the lives of teens, the present-day decadence is your handwork. You created this monster "baby". Own it.

For almost all delinquent teenagers, going astray, getting involved in crimes and addictions, are not necessarily deliberate choices. As teens they do not make plans to become criminals. A lot of times they are dealt wrong hands by the circumstances beyond them. Most of the time it is the parents and the politicians, who introduce the ill wind that eventually blows them away. But in the long run, they are generally blamed by society. I am not here to defend teenagers because they certainly have some share of the blame. But the bulk of the blame for juvenile delinquency rests proportionately on the adults in their lives. The parents, City Mayors, lawmakers in the State legislature, the state governors and the state attorney generals and district attorneys (DAs) and in some cases, the Congress of the Federal government, have a lot to do with what has gone wrong with society in general and our children in particular. The way laws affecting teens, addicts and felons are crafted by lawmakers and the way these laws are interpreted, enforced or not enforced by lawyers, District Attorneys and Attorney Generals, makes the difference between rescuing, reforming or permanently losing culprits, especially young offenders. The so-called "sympathetic", progressive and liberal Democrats handing drug addicts 'clean needles' is an example of how not to help drug addicts to sober up and become good citizens. Distributing fresh needles to drug addicts in San Francisco, for instance, is nothing but an empowerment to drug addicts to continue injecting dangerous drugs into their system. It is like giving a recovering alcoholic a job as a bartender. Nothing could be more devastating to homeless alcoholics than San Francisco City Council giving beer, wine and vodka daily to homeless alcoholics. But unfortunately, there are a lot of city and state legislators and administrators, who think that aiding and abetting addicts by supplying them with such materials as needles and other drug paraphernalia in kiosks, is progressive and humane. There is nothing humane about making drug addicts more addictive to drugs or alcoholics to drinks. Instead, it is a form of abuse and taking advantage of people who are down and vulnerable. They do what they do based on their political calculation and political temperature gauge. These politicians have no desire to stop these dangerous behaviors. If soft on crime is what is selling in that season, such politicians change their political goal post to be elected or reelected not minding who is ruined in the process. If a minority group complains that there are many people in their community incarcerated, the politician, who is there for his own good only, will start to preach soft on crimes and incarceration to be elected or reelected. He or she will not look at what is the right thing to do for the good of the young people, alcoholics and drug addicts and society. Perhaps that is why some people say that politics is a 'dirty game'. If someone who has a strong conscience venture into the political arena, he or she would likely not win an election but if elected, would be a one timer in politics because he/she is guided by conscience only to do the right thing for the people. We can minimize or stop crime in our society if the powers that control the system become less selfish and think more about teens, the future of the nation. Remember that children are born good and innocent only to be spoiled by adults and politicians in their lives.

DRUG AND ALCOHOL USE IN AMERICA:

As human beings we eat and drink to survive. We eat different kinds of food and drink water and some other beverages to nourish the body. Our nature has within it a measure of food and drink that is beneficial to the body to grow and function adequately. But when human beings overeat or overdrink, especially alcohol or drugs, bad things begin to happen to the body, the individual and of course, the wider society. Such substances go from feeding the body to destroying the body. This is human nature at work. Embedded in man in this regard, is also the ability to know when to stop eating or drinking because man has reasoning faculty and common sense. Reason is the faculty that guides our actions and differentiates us from the lower animals. It imposes on us the responsibility of choosing good or bad actions freely. It is always a choice until we incapacitate the reasoning faculty and become slaves instead of masters of our actions and destiny. In other words, the faculty of reason is a spiritual aspect of us; a share of God in us that directs us to choose good actions and avoid bad actions, if we have reached the "age of reason". We also have "common sense", which is related to reason. It is called "common" because all human beings possess it after a certain age irrespective of class, wealth or formal education. It is not the preserve of the rich, highly placed or highly educated. The age of reasoning (the ability to distinguish right from wrong) is the qualification for possessing common sense. It becomes the "common denominator" for all human beings who have reached the age of reason unless they are incapacitated by any other debilitating condition.

When we, as human beings, begin to ignore the promptings of reason in terms of what we eat or drink, the body loses its equilibrium or balance. Eating and drinking go from being a means of nourishment for the body to becoming agents to kill the body, thereby losing their purpose. When the body is suffering, people trained in medicine, use appropriate drugs to heal the body. Overall, the author of human life, the author of food and drugs has given us the tools to control what we eat and drink. But when we ignore Him, we tend to abuse food and drinks and become alcoholics and addicts. When we neglect the voice of reason and common

157

sense but listen to the voice of the "ego", or the devil, we overeat food and abuse drinks and drugs. Why would anybody (with common sense) over drink alcohol when they know the limit their body can handle? Why would anybody put a dangerous substance or drugs into their system, get "high" and lose their independence? When we abuse alcohol and or hard drugs, we hand over our common sense and independence to those substances. They take over and direct our faculties and our affairs the way the devil wants. Then we become dependent on the evil one, who makes us addicted to the command and wishes of those substances. We can no longer say no to alcohol or drugs. When alcohol and or drugs take over the control of our body, we lose our sense of shame and dignity; we become objects of ridicule, and we wouldn't even notice. It is then that we are not ashamed of how we look, how we dress, what we say or where we sleep. Sleeping in the open air at the street corner becomes normal to us. We have lost it, shame and all. Stealing or prostituting to get alcohol and or drugs becomes normal too. Ordinarily reasoning and common sense regulate human behavior and morality. Since reasoning and morality are of God, a human being acts and behaves according to God's designs which, for believers, means obeying the ten commandments. But for the addict, who is serving imprisonment in the houses of alcohol and drugs, there are no commandments of God. The only being around is the devil, the object of dependence. That is why a drug addict can steal, rape, prostitute and even kill to satisfy the masters. Decadence and lawlessness reign where alcohol and drugs are in charge. These are some of the things we see daily in America today. Were these people born this way? What really happened to them? But do our politicians and government care? That is the question. They don't because their policies are the reason these people turned out the way they are now.

Before alcohol and drugs became more prominent in the lives of Americans, there was a stricter law and order in America. Drunkenness and drug use were not at all common. Smoking and drug use were minimal and limited by certain societal boundaries. Yes, there were societal boundaries then. Those bad habits were generally within the confines of a few men whose bad habits were despised by everybody; teens and women were sheltered and insulated from excessive drugs and alcohol use by those societal customs and boundaries. Moreover, the amount of drug abuse in America then was not problem enough to be focused on in the forties and fifties. They were not worth talking about because they were inconsequential. Moreover, some of these bad habits were picked up by some men as residues of war. People in that age were so God fearing and family oriented that alcohol and drugs did not take away their independence because they still had a solid connection to God, reason and common sense. Respect for elders and people in authority was still highly esteemed. Children respected and listened to their parents. And there were things a teenage boy would not say to the hearing of adults and especially his mother and sisters. Most of the people in authority then behaved themselves most of the time and there were not many scandals. The First Amendment rights had not been abused and bastardized by lawyers and judges in the pursuit of money. There was no "political correctness" at the time. People had a sense of shame and cared about self-respect and human dignity. People's property was respected. Rape was not fashionable because women were respected.

All that went out of the window with the advent of the sixties with "The stone-wall Revolution" and the "Hippie Culture". The Sixties, the Gay and Lesbian culture and the "Summer of Love"- "Woodstock", ushered in the reckless use of marijuana and LSD among young people. Since then, the use of alcohol and drugs in the United States has been having a steady upward movement in recklessness and lawlessness. Right now, it has reached what can be described as a saturation point. It has permeated almost every family and school including grade schools. The greed for money and positions of power have exacerbated the epidemic of loss of God and reason in our society. Today, crimes, depression, suicide, homelessness and untimely death of our very young people through overdose and suicide have become the norm instead of an exception. All this is of our own making and could be avoided if the adults in the room were responsible.

Women embarked on the crusade of "Women Liberation". In the Sixties women thought that adopting all the bad habits which some men got from the warfront was a sign of women's liberation - doing everything men do. Smoking cigarettes, cigars and drinking alcohol was cool and the way to go to "belong". Discarding dresses and wearing pants and looking masculine became common and fashionable among women. Drinking in bars qualifies a woman as mature, liberated and a woman of the sixties who does not need a man in her life. Sooner or later, one does not only see staggering and drunken men in bars and streets after 1:00 am, when the bars close, but also a sorry sight of drunk and staggering women in bars and on the streets as well. Womanhood lost something precious - respect. Chivalry and respect for women started to evaporate gradually but steadily as a sign of freedom and equality.

Women fell prey to rapes and other kinds of degradation because of their conscious and deliberate choice of mingling with men while they are in vulnerable and dangerous situations and positions. Soon some of the women surpassed the men in smoking and drinking. Women liberation became popular in some quarters and among students. Unscrupulous politicians cashed in on that vulnerability and carved out a constituency out of a bad situation. Soon a lot of these ladies graduated from alcohol to smoking cigarettes and cigars to marijuana and of course, cocaine, if one has the money or crack-cocaine, if one is poor. Black women joined this bandwagon to belong and feel free. In many cases these benign habits upgraded into alcohol and drug "dependence", man, woman, rich and poor. The cycle of selfishness and dependence has begun. But who is taking care of the children at home when the woman is on the street, drunk? That is a good question. Children started to raise themselves and now we are seeing the results of that liberation on the streets, in the classrooms, even in the halls of Congress today. Eventually all this dangerous behavior paved the way for the proverbial "like father like son"; "like mother like daughter" situations in the years after. When we have substance abusers in the house, what do we expect of the children in the house? Crack mothers gave birth to "crack babies" without "fathers". Children normally imitate their parents and adults in their lives. That is one of the things that brought us where we are today; under these circumstances America is no longer in charge in a lot of ways because we have lost control and freedom.

Why would a teenager want to put a dangerous substance in his or her system? Stupidity! For the first group of young people who got addicted to drugs or died of drug overdose in America, one could say that unfortunately they died not knowing about the bad effects of such drugs. But what would be the excuse for millions of Americans, young and old, who are still involved with dangerous drugs today? It is hard to defend. Recently millions and millions of young Americans have died of Fentanyl overdose, a deadly drug coming from China through the Southern border into the United States. What would be the excuse for that? Despite all the warnings against fentanyl, our young people are still dying everyday of fentanyl overdose. Is this ignorance, "freedom" or stupidity? In my opinion, I think it is the stupidity of the teens who have seen that fire burns and still choose to put their hands and heads into the fire. In some ways the cause of our children experimenting on gateway drugs, cocaine and now fentanyl could be traced back to our legislators decriminalizing some drugs. The introduction of young people to gateway drugs by our politicians started them off on an addiction path that naturally leads them to the next available poison. That was when they disconnected commonsense and became slaves. As slaves to drugs, they have become obedient to the master even when the next and recent master is fentanyl. But the fact that the very young and naive children continue in this dangerous enterprise is the tragedy of our culture of permissiveness. These casualties are mostly young students. They start with smoking cigarettes as a cultural heritage launched even before they turn eighteen. They follow the culture around them. What does that say about our schools, school administrators, politicians and government? What are the priorities of politicians and the government for our children? It is almost like we, as a nation, want our children to try every dangerous thing to see if they live or die. The national mentality on this subject is reflected on the management and discipline in American schools. Discipline for our children is not a priority and unfortunately it is a deliberate decision by our politicians.

All over the world elementary and High school students are each known by discipline which starts with making them wear uniforms. Psychologically students begin to grow with obedience to authority and elders and learn to follow rules. Such discipline is there for a purpose; it is there to mold character and set boundaries at an early age - dos and don'ts. From the external clothes, discipline and what is embodied in the curricula, students learn that there are certain things they are not allowed to do in school and outside of school. Good governments make sure that the behavior instilled in the school is reinforced at home by parents. By the time they are done at that level of their education, they shall have understood the dangers of drugs and alcohol. It is after they have this formal structure that they can withstand and survive college life. As a culture it seems that we have decided to ignore the lessons of history and the experiences of adults and those who have gone before us. Now we want every child to make their own mistakes first. But unfortunately, many have died in the experiment and others have become slaves to alcohol and drugs into adulthood. Now we must live with a stupid experimentation introduced by those in power.

At the beginning of this topic, we highlighted the cause of illicit drug use. Very related to that is the absence of God in a people's life. Heaven is a place of order and where there is no reign of God, there is no order. The presence of disorder is an invitation to the devil, who is the master of disorder in all sorts of ways. One will inevitably see the disconnect and mismanagement in families and the governing class because there is no law and order. Chaos reigns supreme because there is no order. With respect to order in society the most vulnerable are always the youth and that is why politicians, and the government should make adequate and solid arrangements early to secure the future of our vulnerable children, who are the future of the nation. Family and school breakdown will give inordinate freedoms to the young people, who will run with it and justify every bad behavior as an exercise in freedom. It is the duty of those in charge to define freedom accurately and appropriately to our young people.

After so many years of seeing people and sometimes close relatives die of alcohol and drug overdose, it is hard to understand how young people still choose to experiment on them. When a teenager attends several funerals of schoolmates, who died of overdose, and turns around and starts experimenting on the same alcohol and drugs, it is now an act of stupidity on the part of the teenager. When a teenager watches a friend or classmate, who died of drug overdose, laid six feet in the grave and he or she does not learn a lesson from it, he or she must be stupid. At that age one is supposed to have enough common sense to run far away from alcohol and drugs. The only other way to look at it will be that the teenager has at an early age lost the faculty of reasoning. That means that he or she has no connection with God; and that would be very, very, tragic. It is that tragedy, when multiplied, that produces the violence that is playing in our schools, streets and society today. Apart from our veterans on the streets, who have wartime issues, the rest of the population, who are homeless, doing drugs, and committing suicide, come from the tradition described above. And the picture does not speak well of us as a nation. America has been blessed by God to do anything; achieve any goal she puts her mind to. But America lost her innocence when she put her back on God and is now facing the devil who is at work in our society today. That takes us back to the family, the government, the lawmakers, school boards and school administrators. Some or a number of these institutions have dropped the ball because a good number of our teenagers have lost their independence to these substances so early in life when there were no "adults" in the house to help and direct them. Where there is no father in the house or where an alcoholic or drug addicted mother in the family failed them, their government has doubled down on the same failure to a third degree of comparison. There is something substantially wrong when custodians of a nation give authority to teenagers to have free sex and if pregnancy results, to kill the baby in the womb; when the mindset of a teenager can be messed up to a degree to shoot up his or her school and take his or her life after; when there is a government approval for a man to marry another man; when a nine year old boy is given permission and encouragement to change his sex to female even when, at that age, he has no idea what it is to be male or female. The way these anomalies in our society today are backed up by "adults in the room" can even make a teenager start drinking or doing drugs. Yes, there is a big, big problem in the Republic. The frequency of these killings in schools and on the Nation's streets, has desensitized the conscience of the killers and the people in authority. These teen and youth behaviors of revolts after the loss of their innocence, can be traced back to the kind of schools they attended. And that is another tragedy.

TEEN SUICIDE:

Suicide among our young is on the increase. The sorry thing about it is that these young people are just beginning life and ending it abruptly. They are students for the most part and have no financial or family obligations; most of them enjoy room and board under their parents' roof and have only their studies to think about. Ordinarily they have no reason to take their own lives at that stage of their life. In an article written by Sandy Cohen, a Senior writer for UCLA Health quoting Dr. Carl Fleisher of UCLA, in California wrote:

"Suicide is the second-leading cause of death among people age 15 to 24 in the United States of America. Nearly 20% of high school students report serious thoughts of suicide and 9% have made an attempt to take their lives, according to the National Alliance on mental illness."

This is very unfortunate. The question is: what would make a high school student want to take his or her life? About sixty or seventy years ago, one could hardly make that claim. So, what has changed? Society has been changed by our political elites, one would say. Sixty years ago, in America suicide was only seen among adults, who were ex-military; or among people who were frustrated because they could not take care of themselves or their family because of work or financial problems. It was about people who lost hope and gave up. Even then it was rare, very rare. But what is the burden or responsibility of a High School student that could push him or her over the edge to commit suicide today? It was unheard of that 15- to 24-year-olds, who are supposed to love life, out-going, with a bright future ahead of them, would think of committing suicide. But according to Dr Fleisher, "teenagers and young adults have had rising rates of suicide compared to 10 or 15 years ago. The things that make them vulnerable are where they stand socially and where they stand developmentally. Developmentally, their judgment and decision-making abilities are still coming online. The prefrontal cortex - the brain's executive control center - doesn't fully develop until one's mid-20s."

What is then the cause of suicide in this age bracket? Depression, loss of hope, and mental illness! To take one's life requires some degree of hopelessness and lack of control because we are naturally selfish and love to live. But what pushes someone to that edge, is the main question and problem? I think it goes back to the most fundamental thing human beings have or should have. It is the acquisition of healthy reasoning, and judgment which come from our Maker. The ordering of reasoning ascribes the origin and end of life to that Maker; we commonly call God. So, when someone is well-anchored in God, reasoning and common sense dictate that one does not have the right to take one's life as in suicide no matter what. We know that reason and common sense have been given by

God to every human being at a certain age irrespective of social class. So, for someone to commit suicide one must have a disconnect with reasoning. What causes this disconnect? This disconnect could be caused by many factors.

Firstly, if someone does not believe or has stopped to believe in God, one can reach a point in one's Live's journey or adversity that one can end it all by suicide. Secondly one could also alter the functioning of the brain through substances. When reasoning is diminished through drugs or alcohol, one is no longer in charge and anything could happen. In our most recent history, apart from drugs and alcohol, teens have been inundated with transgender issues in school, issues which are beyond their capacity; they have been, and in some cases officially, taught to hate other races thereby making the school's environment toxic and hostile; they are indoctrinated to do things that their undeveloped minds could not cope with at that age. But since they are willing to do or try anything, they jump headlong into situations they don't quite understand. But when they look back at their actions, they regret what they have done. When they fully understand the implications of what they have been drawn into by adults and they cannot take back the bad decision, some of them are depressed and hate to continue living. Such could make a teenager see suicide as a way out, especially if they don't have a strong anchor in a Supreme being. A very strong distrust in authority figures who have pushed them into such bad decisions instead of leading them the right way, could trigger a suicidal thought or actual suicide in young people.

Thirdly a good number of Americans no longer believe in God and this attitude has rubbed off on the young people. When parents do not strongly believe in God and have no religious practice which the children could emulate, young people could take scandal from that. Consequently, their children have no spiritual bearing most of the time. They may practice some religion here and there and off and on. During the turbulent teen years, these young people, who are uninformed, delicate and very vulnerable, have no sustained spiritual anchor or direction. That situation alone could become a recipe for disaster when they run into trouble. Imagine such a teenager meeting the first 'roadblock' of life. It will be so overwhelming and threatening that his giving up on people, school and life would be very easy. After all there would be nothing good to live for in a world that is nothing but frustration, depression, pain and lacking in meaning. There would be no one to run to for anchor or for direction. The teen would build a wall around himself and not open to anyone. Since there is no trust and no hope or meaning in life according to his very limited reasoning, he would not confide in friends and parents until he does the unthinkable - suicide. God is the only Hope and cushion in times of trials, depression and pain. Spiritual anchor in God is very important for parents to inculcate in their children to build a better society where teenagers will not become vulnerable to suicidal thoughts.

We know that lack of knowledge or insufficient knowledge can interfere with one's reasoning. We have already seen that it is true that the brain which controls reasoning can be altered through alcohol, drugs or indoctrination. When politicians and legislators at the local, state and federal levels, indoctrinate teenagers through bad legislation which affect young people and enforce those laws for whatever reason, the effects come back to bite that society in the rear through the actions of young people. Some politicians have only their political career in mind when they legislate. They only know to follow the favorable political wind to win elections and reelections by doing the will of the donors. Some of the laws help teens to be entrapped in the vicious circle of alcohol and drugs which can enable some teens to become homeless or even commit suicide. When this happens, their blood will be on the heads of those adults who either put them in those situations or were enablers. No regular teen, who has a good parentage and benefits from the good laws and good advice of politicians will ever think of committing suicide. It is adults who misdirect teens.

Nowadays people, including these politicians, are asking why students and young people are violent and suicidal. A few decades ago, that was not the situation. Some things have changed in the political climate of the country and the way our children are raised today. Adults have raised people who have become monsters to themselves and to society. While some blame goes to them, a big chunk of the blame goes to the adults in their lives in a lot of ways. Let the truth be told; the government has a lot to do with what has happened to the children more than their parents these days. Some government administrations and politicians use their power to handcuff parents through laws and execution of laws to influence how parents raise their children. Some administrations usurp the God-given power parents have or should have over their children. This is abuse of power. Unless a parent is under the influence of drugs or is insane, no one can love and take care of a child more than the parents. But when the government forcefully usurps this naturally given function from parents and gives it over to the school, the results are what we see in the homes, schools and on the streets of America – violence and suicide among our youths. They kill others randomly and kill themselves as well.

CHAPTER FOURTEEN: HOMELESSNESS IN AMERICA

All over the world, people, for a variety of reasons, experience homelessness. Ordinarily nobody likes or chooses to become homeless voluntarily. It is also true to say that people don't wake up one morning and become homeless. It always follows a pattern or sequence of events which progresses into that day that an individual has no roof over his head, and he becomes homeless. Naturally human beings like and enjoy the comfort of a good surrounding or a good house or apartment they can call their own. Moreover, there is a certain pride that goes with the ownership of a place people call home. So, why do people end up becoming homeless? In fact, a bigger question is: why would anybody in America, the richest country in the world, become homeless? But the reality is that there are about 600,000 homeless people in the United States of America. This embarrassment has been with this country for a while, but it has gone out of control lately. The only reason this writer is dealing with it now is because the situation is getting worse despite the enormous amounts of money spent on homelessness by the federal, state and local governments as well as religious and charitable organizations in the country. What are the main reasons people become homeless? Each case of homelessness is different. Homelessness can be caused by:

1. Divorce

2. Housing shortage

3. Unemployment

4. Family breakdown

5. Physical or mental illness

6. Drug/alcohol abuse

7. Domestic violence

8. Teens not feeling safe at home.

Notice that the causes mentioned above are all man made. And that is the tragedy of homelessness. When people become homeless, some of them sleep in their cars or vans at the early stage of their homelessness; some sleep under bridges or on the streets, while some live in uncompleted houses and battle with seasonal and nightly elements. Some homeless people build make-shift shelters to minimize excessive rain, heat or cold. While homeless conditions are uncomfortable, the above reasons why someone could become homeless are not equal. Some conditions are temporary while others are more addictive and permanent. There are varying degrees and reasons for homelessness. A housing shortage, unemployment, family breakdown, and divorce situations may not be as long lasting as mental illness caused by alcohol or drug addiction would. It is homelessness caused by mental illness that we are mainly going to deal with here.

Homelessness is bad enough. But with the amount of money the nation puts into homelessness and housing every year, the number of homeless people should be going down. But unfortunately, the opposite is the case. That seems to suggest that the solution of homelessness in our country goes beyond money. In a two-year period, California alone spent 4.8 billion dollars on homelessness; New York spent 3 billion dollars in 2019. These amounts of money have not changed the homeless situation in these States. Why? The homeless epidemic is growing in some states more than in others. That means that something else is going on. To get to the 'why' we need some more information. According to the latest statistics from the Department of Housing and Urban Development:

1. California accounts for 171,521 homeless people;

2. New York - 74,178;

3. Florida - 25,959;

4. Washington - 25,211

5. Texas - 24,432.

If one listens to some politicians who are talking about ending or minimizing the number of homeless people in their campaign trips, one will constantly hear a cry for more money. But we already know that what mostly causes homelessness is mental illness, which is caused mainly by bad administrative policies, which are mainly responsible for failed schools, drug and alcohol addictions which develop into mental illness. The other factor worth mentioning here is the traumatic experiences of a small number of men and women who were in combat. Some of our veterans come home with post-traumatic stress disorder (PTSD). This condition puts them in situations that make them unable to function optimally to hold jobs or maintain healthy relationships; it can make them do things that land them into prisons which, in some cases, exacerbate their mental problem. Several past government policies did not do right by these veterans. Various governments have sent young men and women to wars and when they came back with the scars and ravages of war, the government barely gave them any attention. The way the government and people have treated them worsens their mental problems and becomes a good recipe for homelessness in that population. The Vietnam war veterans were the first to experience this humiliation and abandonment. They were abandoned and in some cases were disgraced by the government and people who sent them to war.

For these homeless victims, veterans and others, a good place to start would be to offer a completely mandatory, free, mental, drug and alcohol inhouse treatment to all until they are healed enough to function properly in society. There should be no exception to this therapy. After that first and crucial step, the government should make sure that the rehabilitated homeless and homeless veterans would be given or helped to get good accommodation and make sure they can now maintain a good family relationship and to hold jobs. More than enough money has been spent in California already that would have taken care of the homeless through compulsory inhouse rehabilitation. But we know that by their policies, some politicians have never had the will to eradicate the problem of homelessness. They have purposely used all this money to put on "band aid" which were not meant to cure but manage and keep the sale of "band aid" on going. The existence of homelessness creates a perpetual campaign slogan for some politicians to attract government money for their constituency. If homelessness is eradicated, what will be the reason to ask for people's votes? That is how they stay in power. This is a shame and the wrong side of politics.

The next thing to do after solving the problem of homelessness and properly establishing homeless men and women would be for the Federal, State and charitable organizations to join hands to seriously stop young people from considering taking drugs or alcohol at an early age in order to stop future homelessness. That is the big elephant in the room, which nobody wants to touch. It is the same elephant in the room that helps politicians and their agents to keep homelessness as part of a city or state fixture that is there only to be maintained, not eradicated. The same politicians and trial lawyers, for obvious reasons, think that mandatory treatment for the homeless and prohibition of young people from indulging in drugs and alcohol very early in life violate their First Amendment rights. That argument goes only for people who are looking for an excuse or a way to dodge their political responsibility to the people. We all know that all governments mandate things on their citizens all the time if the mandate is for the good of the concerned individuals and the country. If mandating good principles to produce good and responsible citizens is illegal, that would be a very good "illegal" move by the government. Moreover, that would not be the first time the United States government has mandated people to do something. The American government mandated masks and six feet distance during the COVID 19 epidemic for the good of each individual and everybody around them. That was not declared unconstitutional by these politicians and lawyers.

The First Amendment of the Constitution has a context and is reasonable, thanks to the wisdom of our Founding Fathers. It is like a covenant: if you want this you must do that - (a quid pro quo situation). There is no law in the United States that says everyone must drive a car. But the government says: If you want to drive, you must possess a driver's license for the safety of all. It is mandatory for anyone who wants to drive in the States. But no one has said that it is unconstitutional to mandate a license to drive in any of the fifty States. The mandate is to safeguard the lives of drivers and any other person using the streets and highways in the state or nation. Again, to live in any state in the United States of America and earn an income, the State and Federal governments mandate that one pays State and Federal income taxes on what one earns. Even though that is mandatory, no attorney or politician has complained that it is against the First Amendment. If one does not want to drive, one does not have to possess a driver's license. If one does not want to pay taxes, one must not earn any income. If addicts or homeless people want to live in this or that city, they must accept a mandatory and free rehabilitation by the city and vacate the streets and make-shift shelters. This is for the good of all. There is nothing unconstitutional about it.

The First Amendment does not give citizens the license to do everything they want. It is for the same reason that criminals who do the bad things they want, are removed from society and put in prison against their will. Imprisonment deprives them of their right to be in society for a reason - they become a nuisance in society; they are temporarily removed from society to learn how to live well with other people (a kind of mandatory rehabilitation). They lose a lot of the privileges they used to enjoy as citizens. Yet nobody has challenged their incarceration as an infringement on their First Amendment Rights and freedom. For example, everyone in America has the right to choose to like or associate or not with anybody or people, like one's neighbor; but if one chooses not to like or associate with one's neighbor, the First Amendment, does not give one the right to kill that neighbor, for instance, just because one does not like that neighbor. Yes, the First amendment has some limitations. Therefore, if one becomes a nuisance to society, the government has a right to curtail that individual's First Amendment's rights. For example: If an American is abusing drugs and or alcohol to a point that the addiction is affecting the individual's ability to properly function in society by becoming a societal nuisance or threat, the government has a right to mandate that he or she go into rehabilitation for the good of society just as the government intervenes when a person wants to jump from a tall building or a bridge in order to rescue the individual. Sending one for a paid rehabilitation is a way to rescue the individual for his good and the good of the society. It has always been a policy in this country that when an individual's action potentially becomes dangerous to the individual or another person/ society, the government has always waived the First Amendment right of that person to that action. So, it is not a tenable argument by some politicians and attorneys who claim that government mandatory rehabilitation for drug addicts, alcoholics and homeless Americans is unconstitutional. Rehabilitation and follow-up treatments are what the funds allocated by State and Federal governments as well as Charitable and non-governmental agencies are supposed to be used for, not for bureaucracy, politicians and their cronies.

Unfortunately, some people use these funds for other things that do not provide permanent healing of the problem. Every year different levels of American governments and other agencies spend trillions of dollars to eradicate or minimize the number of addicts and homeless people on the streets. Remember the famous "war on drugs" over the years. That war is still raging. But instead of winning the war and eradicating the addiction, the number is increasing every year. That seems to put into serious question the sincerity of these government operatives involved in the war against drugs and homelessness. It looks like some people are feeding on the pain and misery of these addicts and homeless people by making the project profitable in another way. It sure looks like some people's intention is not eradication or victory in the war against poverty, drugs and homelessness. Rather it appears that it is designed to be a recurring management of a disease that keeps the government perpetually involved in a poverty, drug and homeless war fought not to win but a war to keep some people on a steady job with a very good salary. I hope it is not so, even though it smells like it. What we know for a fact is that these States and cities, with a preponderance of poverty, drug addiction and homeless problems, always ask for more money to deal with the same problem every year. The politicians use the crisis to get more money from the Federal government or raise taxes to throw some more money at the problem. We also know for a fact that it is not primarily or necessarily a money problem since all the money thrown at the problem all these years has yielded no good result. Instead, it is a policy problem. To solve this problem, there must be a policy change that will mandatorily put all the addicts and mentally challenged individuals not in prison, but in a treatment center, established and run by professionals until the patients are fit to live in society and on their own.

After the homeless problem the next job of the government is to protect the interest of the people by stopping young people from harmful activities to themselves and the society. The future of our nation is the young people of our nation. They deserve anything we can throw in to give them a better life than we have enjoyed. Talking about life, we did not do badly at all. Looking at where some of our young people are today in terms of self-destruction, we, the adults, have a lot to chew on. No price is too much for this venture. We can and should throw in all we have to reevaluate how we are raising and treating our children, the only human asset we have. If we do right by them as they are growing, we will not have to worry about suicide, drugs and alcohol addiction or homelessness in future. It is ironic that other countries which do not have one third of the resources we have, don't have drug and alcohol addiction and homeless problems as we have, not even in most so-called third world countries. As Americans we can do better than what we have done now if governments and lawyers could go back into the minds of the Founding Fathers, who had God as the foundation of their lives and the nation they founded. God was part of their foundation.

So, why do our politicians and trial lawyers use the First Amendment as an excuse for not aggressively stopping young people from embarking on dangerous enterprises as well as not giving aggressive treatment to mentally ill patients, who eventually become homeless? It is all about money, the almighty dollar, for trial lawyers and "politics" for politicians. Who really believes that a drug addict, an alcoholic or mentally ill patient will like to go to a home for rehabilitation willingly? I am sure no one does, not even the politicians. The addict knows that there will be no alcohol or drugs in the rehabilitation home. One doesn't need a degree to know that. Rather everybody knows that these people have a problem called "addiction"; they are not in control of their lives and actions. That means that they are not in complete control of most of their actions when it comes to the object of their addiction. Yet our politicians, in the name of the First Amendment, give them the right to decide if they want treatment or not, just as the same politicians and attorneys have given nine-year-olds the right to choose to be boys or girls. These same elites would not let a nine-year-old drive or drink alcohol. But for drug and alcohol addiction which result in mental illness and homelessness, politicians should re-examine their consciences to see if they are really fighting for the people in their constituencies or for themselves. Some politicians, by their actions and the laws they pass, promote indiscipline in school, encourage student dropout and overall lawlessness. It is our politicians who make excuses for the young people, who eventually start smoking and doing drugs at a very early age. They make light of young people stealing in shops by calling it "shoplifting" and no punishment is required. As young people, they think it is okay to steal in shops. They legitimize "gateway drugs" and excuse offenses, house-break-ins and vandalism by minors in minority and poor neighborhoods just to win elections. Incrementally these young people lose their bearing and follow the wrong tracks in life. The excuses by politicians help to make young people become losers, public dependents at an early age and those excuses definitely prepare them for different crimes, drug or alcohol dependence. To maintain their drug habits, these young people specialize in other crimes like stealing, lying and murder. The poor mental state and health of mental, drug and alcohol addicts make them lose value, self-consciousness, self-worth and dignity. That is why some refuse to stay in shelters. For one thing they are not stupid; they know that they will not continue their drug habit in rehabilitation and treatment centers. Moreover, they believe that it is better for them to sleep on the street with their "fix" than to sleep in a comfortable rehabilitation center without it. That is how we developed poor neighborhoods where our politicians visit every election year with promises that they do not mean to fulfill.

POLITICS AND HOMELESSNESS:

Why do we link homelessness with politicians and politics? Politicians are elected by the people with a mandate to serve them for a period. At the end of the term, the politician shows the electorate what he or she has done for the term to make them better or worse as a people. Good governance is characterized by the good life of the people who elected those in government. Areas of evaluation would be: is there peace and prosperity in the area in question? Do people have good jobs, peaceful streets and neighborhoods etc? If there are, the individual politician has fulfilled the mandate and has earned reelection. But if there is chaos on the street and everybody is afraid to come out because of gangs and bandits because there are no jobs for people, the politician has not fulfilled the mandate. If the shops are closed because of shoplifters, looters and homeless people, the politician will be blamed for them. The evidence of the politician's work is the state of his City, State or Country at the end of his or her tenure. The policies of some politicians have contributed to the increase of homelessness in many cities and states of the United States.

We saw some statistics above regarding some states with the highest number of homeless people in the nation. There is a correlation between crimes, homelessness and the people in charge in those Cities and States. The condition of the city or state all points to good or bad governance on the part of the politicians: president, governors, district attorneys, mayors, state and federal legislators in those territories. In that mix not all the politicians will be at fault. It all comes down to the policies adopted by those in power. Some cities and states will be doing well because of their policies while others will not on account of their negative, liberal or progressive policies. That is precisely why we make comparisons between cities and states run by a political party or another. For instance, we saw above that the state of California has about 171,521 homeless people on the street, while New York has 74,178, Florida has 25,959, Washington has 25,211 and Texas has 24, 432.

Statistics show that, on average, 55 people became homeless in the United States every day in 2023. It also shows 10 states with the largest homeless population per capita.

1. California Population 39,455,353: Homeless 171,521

2. Vermont Population 641,637: Homeless 2,780

3. Oregon Population - 4,207,177: Homeless 17,959

4. Hawaii Population - 1,453,498: Homeless 5,967

5. New York Population - 20,114,745: Homeless 74, 178

6. Washington Population - 7,617,364: Homeless 25, 211

7. Maine Population- 1,357,046: Homeless 4, 411

8. Alaska Population- 735,951: Homeless 2,320

9. Nevada Population- 3,059,238: Homeless 7,618

10. Delaware Population- 981,892: Homeless 2,369

By cities, this is the list of 17 highest homeless populations in the US.

1. Santa Cruz-Watsonville, CA.

2. Salinas , CA.

3. Santa Maria-Santa Barbara, CA.

4. Los Angeles, CA.

5. San Luis Obispo, CA.

6. San Jose, CA.

7. Honolulu, HI.

8. New York City, NY

9. Santa Barbara, CA.

10. Eugene, OR

11. San Francisco, CA

12. Salt Lake City, UT.

13. Turlock, CA.

14. Battle Creek, MI

15. Seattle, WA.

16. Stockton, CA.

17. Springfield, MA.

Out of 17 worst homeless cities in the nation, California alone has 10 cities. The question here is: who are the politicians and mayors and governors running these cities and states with the greatest number of homeless people? Most of them are run by the same Democrat Political Party. This is not a coincidence. That means that it is not the people of the city or state; it is not lack of funds; it is the policy adopted by the politicians of a particular party running these States and Cities. It revealed that California is the worst State in the nation as far as homelessness is concerned. It is also known that California is the most liberal and progressive State in the nation. That means that liberal and progressive policies are the main cause of homelessness in America. Next to California in homelessness is the second progressive and liberal State in the nation; and that is New York. In the list above, the worst cities with the homeless population in the country are also in the State of California. That seems to suggest that liberal policies are a big part of the problem of homelessness.

It is a fact that the Democrats have been running the affairs of the State of California for a very long time now. The last Republican Governor of California was Arnold Schwarzenegger after the recall of Democrat Gray Davis. Governor Schwarzenegger served the remainder of Davis's term and did his own term from 2003 to 2011. Before this time, the last Republican Governor of California was Pete Wilson from 1991-1999. Under him California enjoyed part of the good old days after the great presidency of Ronald Reagan, one of the greatest presidents that America has produced. The city on the Bay, San Francisco, has been run by Democrat Majors forever. Among other crimes, San Francisco has a very large homeless population. How do the Mayor and City Council members handle homelessness and alcoholism in San Francisco. It has been customary that the city of San Francisco has been distributing fresh needles to drug addicts for many years? They did not stop there. According to the Daily Mail:

"The city of San Francisco is handing out bottles of beer, glasses of wine and shots of vodka to homeless alcoholics - and spending $5 million a year on the program," reported James Gordon for Daily Mail. Continuing he said:

"The alcoholic drinks are served by nurses as part of the city's 'managed alcohol program', which has been running for four years, as a way of taking care of vulnerable homeless people. Nurses assess patients and typically serve the equivalent of 1-2 drinks between three and four times a day - handing out either 1.7 ounces of vodka or liquor (about a shot), 5 ounces of wine (a glass) or 12 ounces of beer - about three-quarters of a pint. Experts involved in the program say that it has actually helped to keep alcoholics out of hospitals, jails, and even from dying".

As you can see, this is rehabilitation, San Francisco style. Do sane people cure alcoholism with more alcohol? These are politicians. Only in the liberal city of San Francisco! This is the policy of politicians to eradicate alcoholism among the homeless people of San Francisco. After four years spending $5 million a year ($20 million in four years) on the program, the alcoholics are still there and the homeless are still there. What progress, San Francisco! Bad policy, bad outcome!

It has been the same party, the same Governors, the same State majority Assembly and Senate in California for decades now. The mayors of most of these California cities are all Democrats and ironically some of them are from the minority groups and neighborhoods, which are negatively impacted by the bad policies. Politicians from poor neighborhoods treating their people this way! Is that all they can show all those years? Apart from homelessness the States of California and New York are the worst in other crimes in the nation for the same bad policies. All that notwithstanding, California District Attorneys (DAs), do not enforce the laws on the books, because they are elected with funds from liberal and atheist George Soros, who does not want the laws on the books enforced. Hence almost all the cities in California and others run by George Soros' DAs are crime-ridden. It is like when the inmates are left to run the asylum. In these cities criminals control the streets. When the police refer criminals for prosecution, the DAs release them. The Democrat policy is designed so that criminals get all the guns they want illegally while law abiding citizens are handicapped legally to own guns. The same thing can be said about the States of Vermont, Oregon, Hawaii, New York and Washington, just to name a few. It is the policies adopted by the political elites in these States that bring about crimes and homelessness as well as lack of prosperity for the people. If you look through the states and cities where there is a large population of poor people, you will see that it is run by the same people and Parties promising handouts to people every election year. Year in and year out, there are no good schools, no progress, no prosperity, no growth, no jobs for the young people. The people in these areas are just trying to survive amid looting and gang enterprise. The little economic activity left in the cities is chased out by looting of the stores by desperate young people from poor neighborhoods. In the liberal Democrat city of Washington D.C, about fifty-two (52) businesses have relocated to other cities because of regular and consistent carjackings, robbery, killings, store lootings and general disruption of law and order because the politicians adopted the "defund the police" policy in 2022. The police funds and the Police force in these areas have been slashed seriously. That makes it difficult to respond to 911 calls to come to the help of the people in those cities. In the absence of police, the criminals took over control of the cities. Unfortunately, it is the poor in those cities that suffer the consequences. The rich do relocate and the politicians, who defunded the police, have the benefit of official police protection paid for by the taxpayers plus their private bodyguards. They can afford them.

Here are some of cities that have "defund the police" policy and the amount defunded:

1. San Francisco, California ($120 million);

2. Portland - Oregon ($16 million);

3. Seattle - Washington ($3.5 million);

4. Oakland, California ($14.6 million);

5. New York - New York ($1 billion);

6. Washington DC ($15 million);

7. Baltimore, Maryland ($22 million);

8. Philadelphia - Pennsylvania ($33 million);

9. Salt Lake City, Utah ($5.3 million);

10. 10. Hartford, Connecticut ($1 million)

11. 11. Norma, Oklahoma ($365,000);

12. 12. Austin, Texas ($150 million);

13. 13. Los Angeles, California ($150 million).

Do me a favor, what political parties run these cities? Some exercise for you!

The city of Minneapolis is even proposing to disband the police altogether. What is common to all these cities? They are all liberal, progressive cities run by Democrats. The "defund the police" policy has been nothing but a disaster. It does not matter how much money you put into bad policies; the result will have to be bad outcomes of crimes and homelessness. The money will be used to run the bureaucracy, which asks for more money year in year out without any results for the victims of these bad policies. Meanwhile the bad actors are feeding off the bad policies, which MUST continue to exist for them to exist as well.

HOMELESSNESS, CONGRESS AND PORK:

There are three branches of government in the United States, The Executive Branch; the Legislative Branch; and the Judicial Branch. The three branches exist for the good of all Americans. As we have noted above, a lot of the problems that Americans experience these days seem to come from the political class and the laws they pass and the way they run Congress. Among the homeless people in America, we know that a good number of them are veterans. Ordinarily it would be unheard of that men and women we sent overseas to fight to protect us would come home and become homeless while Congress watches. It is a shame on the nation that men and women who protected the nation at home and abroad would be left to languish in poverty, hopelessness and homelessness while the Biden administration is only concerned about the proclamation of "Transgender Day of Visibility" (TDOV). That neglect is why veterans between the ages of 18 and 34 commit suicide. We are too big as a nation to let that continue to happen.

The United States Department of Veterans Affairs estimates that between 2017 and 2020 veteran suicide rates were 1.57 to 1.66 times higher than suicide among nonveteran population. In 2020 alone 6,146 veterans committed suicide which is like 16.8 suicides every day. For a country like the United States, that is unacceptable considering the wealth America has. When these men and women come back, they suffer from several things. Some are maimed - no legs, no arms, no eyes; some have their limbs but carry all kinds of psychological problems - traumatic head injury; some, on top of all these, have no families that care. Divorce is very common in this population. They become depressed; they start drinking and doing drugs to alleviate the pains of neglect and abandonment and become substance dependents. At a point they think life is no longer worth living for them. Hence suicide. We also have men and women who die in the line of duty with dependent families. The wives and husbands and children of the deceased not only worry about their deceased loved ones who did not come home, they also have to worry about accommodations.

The Veterans Administration (VA) is designated to take care of veterans. But why are there still so many homeless veterans and so many suicides among them all these years? It appears there is something lacking because we see a lot of difference among veterans who are sponsored and helped by Private and Charitable groups all over America. These private groups do a lot better with small private donations than what the VA has been able to do all these years. What is responsible for this very noticeable difference? There is so much success with groups like "Wounded Warrior project", "Tunnel 2 Towers" (T2T), "Veterans of America". These groups give veterans psychological help; they give them hope, shelter and reasons to live and the veterans become happy and productive again. Tunnel to Towers gives free homes to spouses with young children, who lost their spouses in the line of duty or if they had a house before, Tunnel to Towers pays off the balance on the house. They do this for the spouses of Firefighters, all branches of the military and even now for homeless veterans. If private groups which depend on small and unpredictable private donations can make such a difference on the lives of veterans of America, why can the United States Congress not do better with our tax money? It appears the wounded veterans and war casualties are not a profitable "constituency" for some reason. And that's a shame.

Can anyone imagine what good could have been done with all the trillions of dollars wasted by "Congressional pork" over the years? It is laughable how much money Congress people waste every year on needless, redundant and wasteful projects in their constituencies just to guarantee their next reelection. They use taxpayer money to build bridges that go "nowhere" in Alaska and elsewhere. These projects are so ridiculous that legislators hide them in appropriations bills in such a way that most congress people do not see them in 3,000-page Bills which are signed by the Presidents. These are funds that could have made lots of real differences in the lives of veterans, homeless and unemployed young people of America and other causes.

Talking about other causes, we all are familiar with private Charitable projects like "St. Jude's Children Research Hospital", which has Eight Affiliate Clinics all over the United States of America. They specialize in Children's cancer and Research. They are run with private donations from ordinary people.

Next is "Shriners Hospital for Children". This Hospital specializes in children's orthopedic conditions, burns, spinal cord injuries, cleft lip and palate. Shriners Hospital for Children has about twenty-one locations in the United States of America. Through research and treatment these hospitals have cured thousands of children with cancer and other deadly diseases and conditions. The parents of these children do not pay anything for the care, their transportation, stay or treatment of their children. They have done a fantastic job with what they have received through little donations. Can you imagine what good could be done through these projects if all the "pork" of congress were put into good use in taking care of our veterans and children with life threatening diseases?

What is congressional pork? Congressional pork refers to the appropriation of government spending for localized projects secured solely or primarily to direct spending to a representative's district. It is the practice of an elected official leveraging their vote to gain valuable concessions in exchange for political support, such as securing valuable government contracts or infrastructure projects for their constituents. In a lot of ways, it is a way some powerful members of congress bribe some members to vote in favor of their Bill in Congress in exchange for some favor for members' constituents. While this practice may not be illegal, it has been criticized by many as unethical, at least. The most upfront critic is "Citizens Against Government Waste" (CAGW). This group has been documenting government wastes through pork barrel politics since 1991. There have been some politicians who over the years have criticized the pork system in Congress. Citizens Against Government Waste led by Tom Schatz has yearly published government waste in "Congressional Pig Book".

Late Senator John McCain (R. - Ariz.) commended the "Congressional Pig Book":

"I believe this book should be read by every citizen in America. What is done here by Citizens Against Government Waste, in my view, is of the greatest importance. (M)y Constituents...need to have these concrete examples of the way that business is done here in Washington,

D.C. unfortunately and the only way it's going to stop is when it's exposed." April 9, 2002.

"I want to thank your organization, Tom, Citizens Against Government Waste, for their tireless work on behalf of taxpayers. Your resources are invaluable to everyone here in Washington and every American citizen as well that's concerned about where their tax dollars are going."

Then Rep. Ted Budd (R-N.C) April 21, 2021.

There were many other members of Congress who spoke up against pork in Congress apart from late Senator John McCain and Rep. Ted Budd above.

These are:

Senator Joni Ernst (R- Iowa) July 15, 2020;

Senator Rand Paul (R- Ky.) July 12,2019;

Senator Pat. Toomey (R- Pa.) May 13, 2015;

Senator Ted. Cruz (R- Texas) May 7, 2014;

Rep. Jeff Flake (R-Ariz);

Late Senator Tom Coburn (R-Okla) April 14, 2009). All Republicans!

Two other Senators loved pork and expressed their views this way.

"Those peckerwoods don't know what they are doing. They don't. They're not being realistic."

Late Senator Robert G. Byrd (D-WV) July 19, 2001.

"All they are is a bunch of psychopaths."

Senator Ted Stevens (R-Alaska). December 26, 1999. (One Republican, one Democrat.)

On account of these objections to Congressional pork, Congress decided to stop the earmarks and pork for eleven years and of course, started it again in 2022, "first in a favorable vote by House Democrats on February 26, 2021, then by House Republicans, who agreed to restore them on March 17, 2021, and then by Senate Democrats, who followed suit on April 26, 2021. Senate Republicans voted to uphold the moratorium on April 21, 2021, but the agreement was nonbinding, and many of them received earmarks." (CAGW.)

Let us see some wasted dollars that could have been used to help and rehabilitate our veterans and other Americans in critical situations.

In 2022, there were about 5,138 earmarks at the cost of 18.9 billion dollars and in 2023 the earmarks increased to 7,396 earmarks, which cost taxpayers 26.1 billion dollars. Since the beginning of earmarks in 1991, the American taxpayers have spent 437.5 billion dollars in 124, 212 earmarks by Congress. This is a lot of money that could have benefited thousands of veterans and American children with cancer and more. Let us look at a few, just a few of the earmarks, to give you an idea of how ridiculous these can be. We have decided not to publish the names of the Representatives and Senators who benefited from these "pork".

Here are some of the areas where Congress spent money for the earmarks. In 2023 alone under Agriculture, Rural Development, Food and Drug Administration, and related Agencies Appropriations Act, 10 legislators received $9,537,427 for eight earmarks funding Broadband expansion for Cumberland and Salem counties in New Jersey; Gustine, California; Washington County, New York; Co-Mo Connect project in Missouri. These projects were unnecessary and redundant because the Federal Communications Commission (FCC) and the American Rescue Plan Act were already funding the Broadband project in the nation. The sum of 800 billion dollars had been appropriated by Congress for broadband in 2022. Other projects were Wheat, Peanut, and Other Field Crops Research Unit facility improvements at the Department of Agriculture's Agricultural Research Services in Oklahoma for $4,117,000; $4,000,000 for Sugarcane Research Unit improvement of Agriculture's Agricultural Research Service in Louisiana; $1,000,000 for infrastructure improvement at the Southeast Poultry Research Laboratory in Athens, Georgia; $500,000 for wild horse management at Nevada Department of Agriculture for two Senators and $117,000 for rehabilitation of a wastewater treatment plant at Dale Bumpers National Rice Research Center in Stuttgart, Arkansas for one Senator.

Other earmarks are $229,551,000 for Edward Byrne Memorial Justice Assistance Grant; $177,880,000 for the Community Oriented Policing Services Program; $13,531,000 for 12 earmarks supporting fishing industries in Alaska; $3,050,000 for modernization and educational programming at New England Aquarium Corporation in Boston, Massachusetts; $7,250,000 for Jimmy Carter Presidential Library and Museum in Atlanta, Georgia; $12,891,800 for 13 Museums including

Universal Hip Hop Museum in New York and Rock and Roll Hall of Fame and Museum in Cleveland, Ohio; $99,659,000 for a physical fitness center annex at Fort Wainwright in Fairbanks, Alaska etc. This is just a small number of the earmarks for just one year to give the reader an idea of the kind of irrelevant issues that Congress is obsessed with mainly because they want the people's votes for reelection.

But the big elephant in the room is the 437.5 billion dollars spent on pork since 1991. Over four hundred billion dollars could be enough money to provide homes to all wounded warriors, the families of warriors who paid the ultimate price, the treatment for drug and alcohol dependents, children's cancer and other deadly diseases and homelessness. This would have eliminated crimes in our streets by more than 80% or more. That could have brought back prosperity and peace in the land. But that would require Congress to do the right thing by allocating these funds to the right places not thinking about scoring political points for themselves. But that is not how the "game" is played in Washington D C. Don't hold your breath.

CHAPTER FIFTEEN: POLITICAL CORRECTNESS

The term "political correctness" refers to language that seems to limit what a person can say about another or a group of people without causing the person or group any discomfort or harm politically. In other words, it is a way of speaking about another or a group by paying more attention to how the message is received or how the language affects another or a group rather than the veracity of the content of what the language conveys. Political correctness is more concerned about how **truth** offends a person or group than the fact that the truth is expressed. Originally the term was used to describe Marxist-Leninist philosophy following the Russian Revolution of 1917. It was used to describe party-line politics. In the 1970s and 80s, it was used to refer to liberal extremism. But today it has taken even a worse turn in this country.

Today in America "political correctness" has become a way to accommodate any falsehood about a person or group at all so as not to offend anybody or group or minority viewpoint. It caters to liberal, fringe or bizarre views to belong and be acceptable rather than the facts that could be offensive to a few. In general, and as a matter of charity or courtesy, a language should try to cause less harm to people around. But it should not take from the fact, which is the reality or truth of what is expressed. When merely pleasing people on political issues to avoid offending anybody (political correctness) takes the place of reality and truth, there is a problem, America. In that situation the truth is shackled and that does nobody any good. In the current American political climate, political correctness is becoming a dangerous tool pushed by the minority gay and lesbian groups, the media and liberal political machinery. It is contributing to political decay and apathy in American society. It breaks down norms, standards and installs leftist relativism as subcultures forcefully shoved into people's throats by the powers that run the government. Any resistance to this madness is labeled with one of the "phobias". The elimination of political correctness from our society is one of the issues that need to be investigated before this nation falls off the cliff. Already subjectivity as a principle, is a big cancer in our modern polity especially for the generation of new socialism and the social media. The danger of subjectivism currently is even higher than has ever been. In a society already very selfish, subjectivism becomes a very dangerous tool in the hands of a generation that really deserves to be called the "me" generation (selfish). The effects of the sixties and seventies account for the moral decadence of the present-day sexual revolution and sexual identity crisis and problems. If we are to continue to be a civilization and a reputable nation, this is the time to rein in subjectivism and go back to objective principles, which deal with reality not phantoms and fantasies.

Objective reality is the principle of truth as God is the principle of life itself. Objectivity is as close as one can get to God because God is truth, the thing as it is, not imagined things, not wished, not relative to anything or subjective to anything, but the unmitigated Truth. But when truth is subjective, it becomes less real and less authentic, with less universal application because it has added an element of relativism and has been individualized and a selfish dimension added to it. So, to get to the real thing, the subjective element must be only in the background for purposes of application to individuals. To let the subjective element take over is to install selfishness which only caters to the self while objective reality caters for the interest of all. The "ego" does not play a big role in objective issues. There are no biases and exaggerations. As human beings, we share an objectivity that applies to all. But when one or a group emphasizes their subjective sentiment, objectivity is diminished, and the society is fractured, and "political correctness" is born. That is why an individual goes outside the universality of humanity and makes individual and private claims of a sexual orientation out of our shared humanity, all to himself. That only attempts to make falsehood into reality.

As far as political issues are concerned, political correctness creates a selfish category for itself and seeks a recognition which tends to impose on everybody else. It seeks to make everybody live by its subjective rules. Political correctness tends to impose the will of the powerful minority on most of the population. For one thing, it is not fair. If the majority resists the imposition, it is labeled "politically incorrect". American political correctness has become a big thing these days because it is peddled by the media, which is overwhelmingly liberal, leftist and subjective as well. Any issue the American media is in front of, becomes a big deal because everybody depends on the media for news. That is the very reason the media should be impartial. The media is not supposed to be like what comes out of the rich Silicon Valley companies like Amazon, Facebook (Meta), Twitter now "X", which are ever ready to cancel anyone who dares to be "politically incorrect". With the media on their side, some minority groups begin to reject the ordinary, normal and objective actions of the majority. To crown it all this whole utopian concept is supported and crowned by President Biden. The leftist billionaire class was controlling national opinion and policy of the nation and had the power to cancel anyone who does not toe their leftist line. This rejection begins to create an acrimonious division and tension in the country. Normal political and civil discussion can no longer go on without bickering and hatred. This is one of the main reasons why the powerful United States of America is sinking in the ocean of Godlessness, immorality, political ignominy and decay, educational decadence, alcohol dependence, crimes, drug addiction, suicide and homelessness. That is political correctness for you.

The media elevated the issues of abortion and the gay lifestyle in the nation to the front and center and if one is not in support of abortion and LGBTQ+, he is canceled and labeled "politically incorrect". The individual's social media posts are canceled by liberal Silicon Valley executives so that nobody hears from the individual or any alternative views. A few short years ago, abortion and gay lifestyles were minority issues and in fact, still are minority issues. But now the media and the political left have made them the big elephant in the room which everybody must worship. They have become the big issues of the day also because the "Obamanesques" government of the day has elevated them to prominence and given them the tools to permeate not only the classrooms and children of America but the entire world.

On the adult level, abortion and gay issues are bad enough but would not be so disturbing because adults can make adult decisions. But when the movement goes as far as becoming issues that the very young and elementary school children must worry about, it becomes highly disturbing and unacceptable. When most of these students are being classified as "politically incorrect" because they refuse to go along with these issues which are being shoved into their throats, the nation should be alarmed and worried. Today school children have been mentally forced to choose between agreeing, identifying and complying with LGBTQ+ issues and having to wear the "politically incorrect", "homophobic" and "transphobic" labels. What a choice for little children sent to school to be educated! That should not be. To be left alone, these children have no options but to go along with whatever those in power want. The problem is that it automatically creates a hostile school environment for the students who should ordinarily be worrying about their studies. The majority dares not question, criticize or raise issues about how killing a baby in the womb (abortion) is nowadays characterized by Democrats as a "healthcare service". One dares not oppose the recently leftist powerful minority without being labeled "politically incorrect" by the media and the minority liberal groups simply because they have the power of the white House, FBI, DOJ and the Courts to harass, detain or punish people. No one dares to defend the right of a parent, who tries to stop a teacher or school from making his or her nine-year-old make transgender and life-altering decision at that age without being called "transphobic" and perhaps prosecuted for "interfering" with the decision of a nine-year-old trans person.

Traditionally acceptable facts, words and phrases are now canceled by the powerful minority. It fits into President Obama's promise to transform America. It becomes "politically incorrect" to say "a pregnant woman" because it would exclude a pregnant woman, who wants to identify as a man. So, they have introduced a more "politically correct" phrase like "pregnant people ", to accommodate a pregnant woman who identifies as a man. The minority wants to replace the term, "women" with "birthing people" to accommodate those women who think and say they have become men. These so-called men are still women because they can get pregnant. To lessen the gravity of the term, "pedophiles" among them, these minority elites now call them "minor attracted persons" (that is adult persons who are attracted to minors); stealing becomes "shoplifting", all to make pedophiles and stealing less odious and "politically correct". That in a way has made the thief and pedophile the victims who should be protected while the real victims have now become the criminals. Pedophiles have now become normal and accepted because they belong to the LGBTQIA+ Community, the minority group which is running the country. Under their regime one can now be sued for using the so-called "wrong pronoun". Can you imagine being sued by a man (he), who looks like a man but thinks in his mind that he is a "she" because you addressed him as a he? These people's intention is to force everyone to deny reality just because they are denying reality. Where is Freedom? How did America come to this? Where has the freedom of an American gone when one cannot call a man a man as he sees him? That is the result of one president's eight years in the White House. America changed.

To get involved in political elections, one must be involved in the so-called political correctness debacle. It has become so common that your typical politician will boldly say things that don't make sense; but because it is politically correct, it is acceptable and highlighted by the media. A conservative politician in a liberal city or neighborhood will say something like this: "As a person I am opposed to abortion, but as a politician I am for and will vote for a woman's right to abortion", just to get votes from people who believe in abortion. That kind of politician is being "politically correct" to win an election at the expense of his conscience, conservative principles and or religious beliefs. It is very convenient to take that position to get into or remain in politics and power. The irony is that this individual knows the right thing to do; but to satisfy his political ambition, he must ditch his conscience, make a wrong judgment in favor of "political correctness". As tragic as it sounds, that is the reality we now face in America. That is one reason America is where it is now. That is why America is losing its position on the world stage too.

Political correctness and the media peddling it will not solve America's problems. On the contrary, it will exacerbate them. If, as a nation and superpower for that matter, we don't change course, there will be more chaos and crime and instability in our cities. Just look at the states and cities which have adopted woke and political correctness principles in their states and cities; young boys and girls are killing one another because they owe allegiance to different gang leaders; there are carjackings, lootings of stores, robberies and killings of innocent civilians on the streets or in their homes. If you think there are too many rapes of innocent women and girls, who were jogging or going about their own business, wait a few more years to let wokeism and political correctness mature fully and perhaps spread more. Does it alarm you that there are far too many young people who commit suicide because they are tired of life which they have barely started? Wait till the newly recruited teenage gays and transgender kids, wake up from the gay and trans dream. Are you surprised that there are fewer and fewer people in America who believe in God today? Wait until the present day gay and trans youths take the mantle of government in a few years. The LGBTQIA+ Community has got some of their members in elective offices. There must be a rethink and retrace back to reality and objectivity and God. As a young man without Faith or God, St. Augustine played around with women like toys as if there would be no tomorrow. He experimented with all forms of immorality and evils of society of his day just as it exists today in our country. But later he concluded in his "Confessions", an autobiography. He wrote:

"You have made us for yourself, O Lord, and our heart is restless until it rests in you."

Every finite thing will pass away. Wokeness, political correctness and all will pass away. But Truth, Reality and God will not pass away.

Man has a purpose in life. There is an innate longing in man for God, solace and happiness. This notion of God, of course, is not politically correct. The quote from St. Augustine's "Confessions" is not politically correct either. Obeying the Ten Commandments is not politically correct. That explains the reason why America is where it is now. That is why America has become a nation where a lot of people can only experience joy, satisfaction and national pride when they look back to the generation that went before. Ordinarily people look to the future for the best. People learn from the mistakes of history and the past and improve today. Parents want their children to do better than them. But in a lot of our neighborhoods today, the parents are taking care of their grown-up's children and grandchildren because the children are out there having children out of wedlock; they are addicted to drugs or alcohol or perhaps are homeless or in prison. Where is the American "DREAM"? There goes the idea of children doing better than their parents because of "wokeism", "political correctness", the bad policies of some people in government. That is also why people are asking how a great and prosperous nation has come to this. How did America come to this? It is sad.

ABOUT THE AUTHOR

The author, Rev. Innocent Emechete, is a Catholic priest, born in
Nigeria, now serving in San Bernardino Diocese, California. He holds a
bachelor's degree in philosophy, two master's degrees in theology and
English Literature, Graduate diplomas in Education, Journalism,
Children's Literature and Guidance and Counseling.

The author has served in the Archdiocese of Los Angeles, the
Dioceses of Sacramento and San Bernardino. He has been Pastor and
Associate Pastor in many Parishes in Nigeria and the United States of
America. He was a Religion and English teacher in High School and
English lecturer in college. Apart from parish work, Fr. Emechete also has
27 years' experience in State and Federal Corrections as a Chaplain
(California Department of Corrections and Federal Bureau of Prisons) in
the United States of America.

OTHER BOOKS PUBLISHED BY THE AUTHOR

1. A Guide to Understanding Romeo and Juliet: Published by FONSAP (Nigeria Ltd) Owerri, Nigeria. 1985.

2. Model English Essays for Secondary Schools: Published by FONSAP (Nigeria Ltd) Owerri, Nigeria. 1990.

3. Entering the poet's Mind: (Some African Poems): Published by Assumpta Press, Owerri, Nigeria. 2004.

4. English As a Second Language, (A Nigerian Focus): Published by Assumpta Press, Owerri, Nigeria. 2004.

5. The Bleeding Iroko: Published by Author House, Bloomington, Indiana, USA. 2005.

6. American Culture And The Nigerian Society: Published by AuthorHouse, Bloomington, Indiana, USA. 2005.

7. The Concept Of The Deity In African Poetry: Published by AYS Press, Ibadan, Nigeria, 2008.

8. What Is In A Name: Published by AYS Press, Ibadan, Nigeria. 2008.

9. Animal Stories Daddy Told Us: Published by Author House, Bloomington, Indiana, USA. 2010.

10. The Igbos And The Hebrew Connection: (The Origin Of the Igbos): Published by Scottessy Publishers, Network Printing Services, Port Harcourt, Nigeria. 2021.

www.ingramcontent.com/pod-product-compliance
Lightning Source LLC
Chambersburg PA
CBHW052130270326
41930CB00012B/2830